UNBREAKABLE

A proven process for building unbreakable relationships with customers

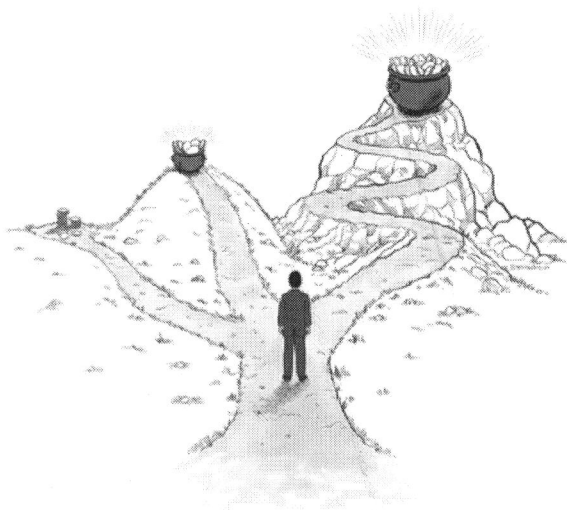

By Jason Ten-Pow

Founder & President

ONR

UNBREAKABLE: A proven process for building unbreakable relationships with customers

© 2021 Jason Ten-Pow

✉ Jason.tenpow@onrcx.com

To request permissions, please contact the publisher at

✉ sweiss@onrcx.com

Edited by John Breeze
Cover art by Matt Ryan
Layout by John Breeze
Illustrations © 2021 by Derek Evernden

Published by CX Publishing House Inc.
Suite 106, 9120 Leslie St., Richmond Hill ON Canada L4B 3J9

www.cxpublishinghouse.com

ISBN 978-1-7776412-0-7

Printed and bound in the United States of America

Dedication

To Ronin,

Dream Big.

Table of Contents

Dedication

UNBREAKABLE

A proven process for building unbreakable
relationships with customers

Foreword

I first met Jason Ten-Pow nearly twenty years ago, when I was on the corporate team at Coca-Cola Ltd. in Toronto, working specifically with McDonald's. Jason, who was conducting online research about new products and new beverage occasions for us, made a strong impression on the entire team on several levels, but from my perspective, he was the first researcher I had encountered who spoke like a marketer and thought like an operator. Meaning—he understood that we had to know more about the customer than our competitors did, in order to truly succeed.

It was the first time our team talked about making decisions based on customer experience (CX)—not just customer perceptions or attitudes. It was the first time we had ever spoken of strategies that were born from the new insights into how a customer bought and consumed our products and how we could apply them to operating better, innovating better, retailing better, and providing better customer service. And it was the first time I saw the financial power of knowing more about customers than just how to reach them efficiently with media, and its consequent impact on sales.

That initial experience of working with Jason—a customer experience all by itself!—imprinted on me and has stayed with me through all my subsequent corporate roles. His guidance to stay focused on the customer, to see them as more than just demographics, quite literally reshaped our Coca-Cola team's approach to decision-making. We had better insights into how customers buy (or don't), how customers find the shopping experience (or don't), how they enjoy the product (or are neutral or, worse, don't), and how they look to the brand for support, help, to complain or repurchase.

Those paths would later become known in the business strategy world as customer journeys—but at the time, I knew that what Jason was designing, researching and analyzing for us at Coca-Cola had larger implications. He was developing a different way of accessing customer insights to make better decisions and then to act on them faster for improved business results. Jason was visionary—and very practical—in how he helped us be more in tune with our customers.

Several years later, I had changed industries and moved to California, where I led marketing for Hilton Hotels & Resorts. Here again, Jason's approach to creating profiles for us to act on the entire customer experience from first considerations and comparisons through bookings and the actual hotel stays came into play. Customer insights helped inform decisions on more than just marketing campaigns; they also inspired customer-based design of interior spaces, common areas, services and amenities and food and beverage, with voice-of-customer research seen as integral to operational strategies and website experiences.

Jason's approach has always been centered on asking the right questions of customers. That's actually the heart of this book—how to ask the right questions of your customers, and how to take the right actions based on all of their experiences with your brand. Jason has honed it into a science, as you'll see, (Read this book!) with practical steps and a realistic understanding of the impact it can make on a brand's success.

Skipping ahead through the years, and after two more corporate roles, I became a Fractional CMO as part of Chief Outsiders, a national management consulting firm. This time, in a prime case of "turnabout is fair play," Jason engaged me, and ONR became my first client. His ask? To help him corral his theories, strategies and approach to CX and turn it into a value-creation system to present to clients.

Jason knew that what he'd created could be an essential tool, a practical roadmap to growth that brands could follow regardless of business, product, or category—and more valuable than straightforward traditional research alone.

Jason's team at ONR conducted the analysis that forms the backbone of this book—specifically, it connects a brand's focus on CX as a competitive advantage with its long-term business results. Turning ONR's foundational research into a strategic approach and practical guide is how this book came to be. Those "how-to's" and "must-do's" turned into the Playbook that is Part III of this book—a step-by-step approach for customer experience transformation.

That's where the idea of this book came from: the "radical" notion that customer experience—married to operational efficiency, service effectiveness, and innovation in products & services—could be a true sustaining engine for business growth, increased sales AND higher customer satisfaction scores and NPS ratings.

Jason invited me to write the Foreword for this book because I preach CX every day as the growth footprint for brands and businesses that are trying to re-establish growth or that are breaking through an inflection point in total size and business performance.

What he might not realize is that I also witnessed him laying the groundwork for that perspective twenty years ago. Back in my Coca-Cola days, when we asked Jason to help us understand our customers better so we could make better decisions, he delivered. Today, with the publication of *UNBREAKABLE*, he delivers again by turning his approach to CX Transformation into a hands-on, practical playbook that anyone can absorb and apply.

Here's the thing: Your customers want more from you—they'll tell you. And as business people, you want more from them, too. So, read up!

"Hey, Jason, you should write a book... " Oh, wait—you did!

KIRK THOMPSON. March 2021

Introduction

Did you know only 6% of brands have actually reached the highest level of CX Transformation and are effectively building unbreakable relationships with customers?

If your brand is one of the other 94% that are aspiring to build deeper customer relationships, then this book is for you.

Prologue:

Our Hero's Dilemma

What brands prioritize ... it's all wrong.

Every story has its hero. Ours is a Chief Executive Officer: intelligent and savvy, a big-picture thinker. As a C-suite veteran, also a capable leader, ready for the challenges that come with the title. Yet despite a distinguished track record, our CEO is in a tight spot: beleaguered, stuck, even stymied! And to make matters worse, they know exactly what the problem is; it's staring them right in their face. The problem—their brand's problem—can be summed up in one word: Prioritization. It's all wrong.

Chasing near-term revenue and profits has taken priority over, well—everything. Meanwhile, creating and sustaining customer relationships—at one time the pre-eminent mission of any self-respecting brand—has fallen so far down their priority list that it might as well be written in mice type. As a result, the balance is off and, inevitably, the emotional connection with the customer has worn thin and the quality of the customer's experience has suffered. The implications are clear: losing sight of the customer as the brand's top priority may well endanger its long-term success.

This is a critical moment for our hero, and an inflection point for the brand. If they choose to take action to re-prioritize the customer, they'll need to make game-changing decisions, engage the entire organization, and evolve the culture. It's a major undertaking. They know that transforming CX has real potential for the brand, and could fundamentally improve its trajectory in the immediate and the long-term. But, will they go for it?

While this CEO may be fictitious, the plight we have described is not. If you are yourself a CEO, no doubt you recognize the situation; this issue must resonate with you. On the other hand, you might see this CEO as delusional, incompetent or even wimpy. Either way, we'd all agree that if the brand is to revive and thrive, it needs help.

(Ø)NR

Part I

Building Unbreakable Customer Relationships

Our customer relationships could be so much deeper, if only we would communicate more!

This book is about relationships—three in particular—and how to make them work unbelievably better. Like many modern relationships, each one is complicated, sometimes troubled, yet bursting with potential. They're also closely intertwined.

The first is the relationship between Customer Experience (CX) and a brand's revenues and profits, a connection so rich with possibility that we've written this book about it.

The second relationship is that vital yet delicate bond between a brand and its customer. At issue is the emotional connection that they once shared and has now been lost.

The third is the relationship between customer data and the brand's actions based on that data, a union with huge upside (if only the two sides would communicate more!).

And what do all three of these relationships depend on to thrive and grow?

The customer, that's who.

Chapter 1

Why Customer Experience Really Matters

As customer knowledge increases, the brand can make more informed decisions and take smarter actions.

CX is the term we use today to describe how a customer relates to a Brand or a business. CX is a reflection of how the customer perceives, reacts to and evaluates a brand based on the sum of all interactions with the brand—in other words, their total experience. The term is literal: it's how a customer "experiences" a brand and if there's one rock-solid, incontrovertible fact about CX, it's this: deep customer relationships that are built on trust and are cultivated to endure are the outcome of good customer experiences—an increasingly rare accomplishment these days, as we, at ONR, have observed in our work with our own clients.

Improving a brand's CX—a transformative process that holds tremendous promise—is a bit like relationship counseling for brands. When successful, it benefits all parties. As experts and advisors in CX Transformation, ONR has worked with a wide range of organizations for over twenty years, helping them to evolve, improve, and deepen, their customer relationships.

Integral to this transformation process is re-aligning a brand's approach to its customer knowledge—basically, it's about improving the way it manages the valuable information that it culls from the data it collects. Customer knowledge is empowering, providing both the insights and the opportunity for a brand to get to know its customer better—much better. As customer knowledge increases, CX Transformation takes place and relationships deepen. The brand can then make more informed decisions and take smarter actions that prioritize its customers and their experiences.

Prioritization—or the lack of it—is the real, underlying issue for most, if not all, brands today. When a brand's focus shifts away from the customer, it loses its *raison d'être*. At ONR, we encourage our clients to implement the re-orientation process that we have developed that helps brands recapture what's been lost over time: the emotional connection with the customer that is at the heart of all strong, resilient relationships. Our approach to CX Transformation is holistic; it's more than an equation, it's a relationship, and we treat it as such.

In many ways, transforming a brand's CX is a return to the brand's core values. Deep customer relationships, almost an endangered species now, was once foundational. It was defined by a shared integrity and a simple acknowledgment that the customer must be at the center of the brand's universe. After all, what's a brand without customers? That's not an existential question, it's a practical one:

No customers = no profits = no brand.

+++

CX is a hot topic today, often the number one issue that preoccupies C-suite leadership in organizations around the globe. It's now widely acknowledged that when CX improves, its benefits can manifest positively and quantifiably throughout an organization. As they realign their priorities, leaders come to realize that it is indeed possible to prioritize the customer at the same time as the bottom line, especially while insulating the brand from economic disruption. When we spoke to Travis Howe, former Senior Vice President, Head of Global Operations & Strategy at The Walt Disney Company, he suggested that prioritizing the customer should be the C-suite's first goal. He further advised brands to formally acknowledge the importance of the customer in their brand's value statement. He then advocated for using this value statement as the brand's "North Star."

A 2018 study by Deloitte (see References) found that "customer-centric firms are 60% more profitable than other firms." Even more telling, Deloitte's research reported that 81% of the brands studied said that in two years' time, they expected to be "competing mostly or completely on the basis of CX." Furthermore, they discovered that companies were "investing in CX at an unprecedented rate."

But will these "unprecedented investments," that Deloitte refers to pay off? Can investments that are intended to improve CX deliver the impact necessary for a brand to differentiate itself from its competitors? Because brand differentiation is what will help businesses remain profitable. In this digital age, consumers already have too many choices, while brands have too few differentiators, and price wars rage on. Even the most customer-centric brands must stay attuned to this reality. No wonder there are only a few CEOs active today who aren't prioritizing CX.

And while the topic may be front and center in the minds of corporate leaders and management gurus, covered in depth by business and marketing media, and hotly debated on LinkedIn, Twitter, and now, by Clubhouse, transforming the Customer Experience remains elusive—for good reason. Getting it right isn't obvious, it's not a straightforward fix. A strong, resilient customer relationship can't be bought, it has to be cultivated.

What the customer is actually looking for, in addition to a product or service, is a feeling of trust; deep, unbreakable trust. At each interaction with the brand, the customer evaluates, sometimes consciously, more often than not, whether they can trust a brand to keep its promises. The strongest customer relationships are built over time when these repeated interactions clearly demonstrate the brand's willingness to consistently meet or even exceed its customers' wants, needs and desires.

+++

It's almost a given that a CEO's mission is to align their brand's actions ever more closely with their fundamental business goals so that revenues and profits continue to increase. The problem is that most CEOs today are under enormous pressures from demanding shareholders and directors, so their all-consuming focus defaults to improving the year-over-year quarterly results year-over-year. Technology is assumed to be the solution to everything. Consumers remain maddeningly fickle. Meanwhile, geopolitical machinations result in completely unpredictable reactions in the world. Then, in 2020, along came COVID-19! Nothing beats a global pandemic for wreaking havoc on the global economy.

Still, any CEO worth their salt, walking into a new-to-them organization on Day One, should be prepared for the challenges that come with the title. They can anticipate the issues; they've seen this movie before. But in thinking about CX Transformation, they also know that their path forward will be constrained by many limitations, the most immediate and urgent one being time. On average, a CEO can count on a five-year term to accomplish what they are being paid well to do. Given the pre-existing pressures, they are already behind on the day they accept the role. They'll need a plan ASAP, one that will deliver timely results, or they risk falling into what we call the "five-year trap".

Here's how it goes. Out of the gate, a CEO has about 12 months to get up to speed, develop a strategy, generate a plan, get it approved and pull the trigger. So, year one is often more focused on planning than actual implementation. On the other end of the CEO's mandate is year five. Realistically, many CEOs are nearing the end of their engagement by this time and have started to check out. The next leader can fix whatever is going off the rails (or take credit for whatever works).

So that leaves the middle of a CEO's mandate—years two, three, and four—to make the most meaningful long-term contributions to the organization they lead. That's about three years to execute that dynamic, resourceful plan and to catalyze change. If they're aiming for long-term impact, they'll need to manage their time effectively. So, while all eyes are still on short-term results, they already know that they need to look beyond and strive to achieve long-term brand success.

This is where these potential limitations on a CEO's term mirror the pressures that brands also face. However, instead of having a five-year window or even a three-year window in which to innovate, a brand has something like a six-month window to start making an impact and producing results. While brands continue to invest in product development to serve as growth vehicles, they face a rapidly shrinking timeframe in which to reap the benefits of that investment. The result: ROI suffers, which is unsustainable by any measure, no matter the nature or size of your business.

+++

In this challenging environment, a newly engaged CEO with an eye on transforming their brand's CX has to make the most of the company's resources, budgets and people. The path forward will largely be decided by their appetite for risk.

First off, the "don't rock the boat" types are not likely to invest in CX. They'll bank profits to keep the shareholders quiet and satisfied. There's not much nuance to this approach; it does nothing for their customers' experience, but it's a safe bet if the top priority is to produce reliable short-term results.

For the majority of CEOs today, the second, and "go-to", strategy is to prioritize technology. In this case, their thinking is that if they keep plowing funds into technology, they can improve the efficiency of their products, services and infrastructure and at least maintain revenues and profits. Along the way, they hope that this will be recognized and appreciated by their customers and possibly improve their relationships with the brand at the same time. At best, it's an oblique approach in terms of CX.

The third path forward is for big-picture thinkers (and our favorite, of course)—CEOs who are committed to transformational change. These enlightened CEOs understand that embracing CX Transformation is an investment in the future. Re-orienting their brand's approach, prioritizing the customer, and re-building the relationship will result in significant and lasting long-term payoffs.

Each of these scenarios has its value, on a relative scale. The first is hardly a bold, visionary move, but it's often viewed as prudent. The second could be seen to be a calculated risk, depending on the technology investment, but it's still relatively safe. The third is compelling; it has great potential, but it requires a much greater commitment of time and resources. So is this third option too crazy-ambitious to consider? In our view, not if you're a strong leader, and especially not if you're ready to awaken your organization's appetite for improvement, transformation and change.

Embarking on CX Transformation is a game-changing decision for a CEO. Corporate directors are generally accustomed to seeing sales and marketing plans for same-store sales growth and campaigns that will increase the customer base. They don't anticipate the extent of the plan that is actually required for CX Transformation. It doesn't fit the conventional mold; in fact, it's a different beast altogether. It calls for a re-alignment of all functions, where teams from every department engage in continuous collaboration. It's a systematic approach with a transformative power that will resonate throughout the organization from top to bottom. Does this sound exciting, challenging, and purposeful, or what?

+++

Domino's Pizza is an example of a Brand that lost its connection with its customers, only to triumphantly rebound. Founded in 1960, Domino's led the pizza delivery sector for decades. They became famous for their promise of "30-minute delivery or it's free!" But by the mid-2000s, Domino's was besieged by competitors, including frozen pizza makers who had upped their game to grab market share. While they had been building their Brand's success on its promise of quick delivery, they had lost sight of what its customers valued most: good taste. It was clear that Domino's Brand-customer relationship was failing; the passion had peaked and sales fell drastically.

It took a dramatic reality check to spark Domino's leadership into initiating a major re-orientation of their Brand to better align with their customers' wants, needs, and desires. They overhauled their operations to differentiate their Brand and used technology to address the specific customer desire to track the status of their orders. They showed their customers that they were listening, and they established an iron-clad, "make-it-right" guarantee that was all about quality and taste. Domino's was able to reclaim its good customer relationships because it took the time to accumulate customer knowledge, share that knowledge across the organization and act on it to deepen relationships. Domino's prioritized the customer. And the ultimate proof of success? In late 2008, Domino's stock price was at its lowest point, just under $4.00 Today, it's above $400.

+++

Straying customers, declining quality, stock price in free-fall; it sounds dire, but Domino's story proves that the brand-customer relationship can be saved; a deep, reciprocal bond can come back even stronger; relationship counseling *can* work!

A successful CX Transformation process has the potential to solve organizational problems and ultimately boost profitability. But before that can happen, a brand must, first and foremost, re-engage with its customers. When a brand solidly demonstrates that the customer is at the center of its universe, trust grows, the bond strengthens, and the customer feels the love.

Chapter 2

The Benefits of CX Transformation

The payoff that deeper customer relationships deliver.

Let's fast-forward into the future for a moment to understand what CX Transformation (i.e. the systematic re-orienting of a brand's priorities so that it more closely aligns with its customers' wants, needs, and desires) can do for a brand. Imagine a mature organization that prioritizes its customers and knows how to consistently deliver experiences that sustain an emotional connection. As a result, deep, trust-based customer relationships have become the norm. What are the measures of success? Well, by studying brands that have attained the highest level of CX Transformation, we can get some insights into this important question.

ONR's proprietary research (as reported in the References section) showed that 88% of those brands that have reached the highest level of CX Transformation reported that their rate of annual revenue growth was above their industry average, and 84% reported that their net profit margin was above their industry average. These numbers are striking: they indisputably demonstrate that building a solid bond with customers can deliver tangible financial results.

What's more, the impact of CX Transformation and the rewards of deepened customer relationships extended beyond just the financial area, showing up in the internal operations of their organizations and creating a significant increase in employee satisfaction.

+++

There was a time when excellent CX was largely the domain of luxury brands. World-class Brands, such as Tiffany & Co, were known for their exceptional customer relationships and one-on-one service. At that level, a Brand like Tiffany empowered the customer to make an extraordinary purchase, possibly even realizing a cherished dream. Together, the Brand and the customer shared the experience. It's those moments that build relationships and exemplify how deeply a Brand can connect with its customers.

+++

What the luxury sector has always excelled in—treating the customer as a VIP, making them feel seen and heard—is now becoming the common playing field for all brands, all categories, all price points. Look at Starbucks; for all of the attention the coffee company amassed with its explosive growth and dominant loyalty program, what was the brand's one true killer app, its game-changer? It was born from the first time a barista picked up a black marker and scribbled a customer's name on a coffee cup. One cup, one customer —from me to you. A brand couldn't get more real, more direct and more personal. With that simple practice, so human and immediate, Starbucks showed the world how to keep customers coming back.

+++

Founded in the 1980s, Costco is another example of a Brand in a category by itself. A warehouse club that brings its members the best possible prices on quality, brand-name merchandise, Costco effectively brought the premium brand experience to the mass market. It's an excellent example of a Brand that is totally focused on making their customers' shopping experiences as satisfying as possible, by offering a wide selection of merchandise, plus the convenience of specialty departments and exclusive member services.

Costco is a prime example Brand that has reached the highest Level of CX Transformation. First, simply by definition as a membership-only retailer, Costco is a customer-centric Brand. It's also focused on the two most regular weekly purchases a person makes: food and gasoline. In-store food sampling and built-out luxury categories are just a couple of membership perks. And because Costco is a club, it can be laser-focused on collecting its members' purchasing data. So instead of offering a wide range of hard goods and staples and hoping for the best, Costco's product range is curated on the basis of information the customer has directly shared with the Brand. It is specifically based on purchasing habits and predictive models, i.e., on customer knowledge.

The difference between companies like Starbucks and Costco and the vast majority of the rest of the world's brands today is obvious: these two brands don't need CX Transformation. A company with customer-centricity already in its DNA inherently values its customer, invests in the quality of its customer knowledge, and knows how to maximize its value. Companies like Costco have customer data constantly at their fingertips, and they rely on it to drive brand-related decisions and actions. These brands are fully focused on matching, addressing, anticipating and guiding their customers' experiences; they don't need a transformation exercise. As Toyota's Ryan Lockwood, Product Owner, Data Platform Connected Analytic Services, told us,

"Customer knowledge needs to be part of an organization's DNA. It needs to be a foregone conclusion."

On the other end of the spectrum are the brands that don't prioritize the customer. They've let their relationships falter; the emotional connection has fizzled, and now they're paying the price. And they still don't recognize that CX is the missing piece of the puzzle. This lack of self-awareness and even self-delusion, is remarkably common.

In our own research, we've found that many brands are falsely confident of the quality of their CX. Of the more than 1,000 organizations we spoke to, 85% of leaders were unable to accurately determine their level of CX Transformation. What was even more concerning was that 97% of brands at the lowest level of CX Transformation thought they were at a higher level. The one bright note is that the research also shows that as a brand progresses through CX Transformation, its leadership's ability to accurately assess their level of CX Transformation does improve.

The fact is that many CEOs are operating with an information deficit. They don't have the data they need to build solid customer knowledge. Where is that data? Even if they have it, it's probably stuck in departmental silos. So it's a double whammy: they lack both the awareness and the actual customer knowledge to make the informed decisions that would result in the best long-term payoff for the brand.

Vinod Varma, of the UnitedHealth Group, notes that many senior executives question why they need to listen to the customer. They believe they already know what the problems are, but the reality is that their understanding is based on their individual biases, their egos, and their desire to lead large organizations. This explains why so many brands revert to quick fixes and cost-savings solutions rather than improve their organization's decision-making process. In Varma's opinion, they don't know the whole picture. As he told us,

"You can't optimize yourself to growth anymore. You can't grow until you grow your customer base, you can't optimize by just lowering costs, you have to create value to retain customers. You've got to solve the customer's problem. I think that all of those factors are playing a role in reinforcing the focus on the customer."

As a starting point, CEOs in this information-deprived state might do well to ask themselves a few basic questions:

- Am I really up to speed on the state of the brand's customer knowledge?
- Do I have a handle on the customer experience?
- Do I know how customers react to the brand at every interaction?
- Are we giving the customer an experience that promises to deepen their relationship with the brand?

It might come as a surprise to you that many CEOs believe they can confidently answer "Yes," to these questions. They believe that solid product delivery is all that's needed to ensure a positive customer experience.

We have news for them: they're wrong!

Part II

There and Back:
Customer Focus Lost and Found

So, where are we, and how did we get here? What caused the disconnect between brands and customers? How, why and when did customer relationships take a back seat to other priorities?

It's an interesting story, and one that will be discussed and debated for years to come. At its core is the progressive series of impacts that we've all seen and felt over the past few decades, not the least of which has been the emergence of digital technology and social media against the backdrop of a financial crisis.

Added to that has been our growing obsession with collecting customer data without a clear understanding of how to make heads or tails of it much less how to convert it into a usable asset that can drive actions that make a meaningful impact on our relationships with customers.

If that wasn't enough of a struggle for brands to wrap their hands around, along came COVID-19: the global pandemic served to sharpen our customers' priorities and heightened their attention to the quality of their experiences with their previously preferred providers of products and services. Where were we when the customer needed us?

Part II untangles these many different impacts and shows how becoming more deeply connected to the customer through the data they provide us offers a viable and valuable way back to discovering what really matters.

Chapter 3

In the Eye of the Perfect Storm

Aligning around the right purpose.

Think back and picture an innovative brand. It's in its early stages of life. As it starts to grow and attract business, its entire focus is on making sure its customers stay connected to the brand in ways that will keep them returning again and again, hopefully with family and friends in tow. From their inception, most successful brands are hyper-conscious of the customer, determined to understand and fulfill their wants, needs, and desires. But with growth come new pressures: other issues start to distract leadership, and priorities change. It's the natural result of responding to the challenges of adapting to a competitive marketplace, and it takes its toll.

This is how brands lose touch with the very people who made them successful in the first place. As they pursue new priorities, their muscle memories deteriorate, making it even more difficult to restore those lost customer connections. In time, the brand shifts its focus to improving organizational efficiency and, as technology beckons, digital solutions start to dominate. Customer commitment is not just assumed, it may even be taken for granted.

There's more to this relationship rupture, of course. For a broader context, let's look at the current business climate. It was shaped by the digital revolution, which set into motion a confluence of disruptive factors—social, cultural, economic. We don't need to review how the Internet changed everything at the end of the last century, how it spawned social networks that up-ended traditional media, completely transforming the way we socialize and communicate. But it's clear that, along the way, it profoundly altered how brands and consumers interact. The digital revolution didn't change the landscape overnight; its effect was cumulative. In many ways, it was a significant contributor to the "perfect storm" that included the 2008 financial crisis and the irreversible impact of social media. Once those clouds cleared, one thing was obvious: brands would have to work even harder to earn back the customer's trust.

Before the 21st century, the brand-customer relationship was straightforward. A consumer purchased a product, gave it a thumbs up and pretty much stuck with it for life. As long as the brand kept up its end of the deal by providing consistent quality, there wasn't much involved in maintaining the relationship, and communication between a brand and its customers was pretty much a one-way street. The brand was in charge.

Brands spoke to customers through marketing in all its many forms. Cleverly crafted messages, designed to seduce and sell, were delivered through tightly controlled channels. As a consumer, if you wanted to deliver a message back to the brand about a product or service, your options were essentially limited to either writing a letter or calling their toll-free number (if they had one!). Your desire to express your thoughts and concerns would usually take you into a frustrating maze from which you'd rarely emerge feeling in any way victorious. In essence, brands controlled the conversation.

With the launch of the first social media platforms, everything turned upside-down. It would be hard to overstate the impact of this development. In addition to connecting with friends on Facebook, Twitter, Instagram or any of the new social media platforms, people started socializing their shopping experiences, communicating consumer-to-consumer. No longer restricted geographically, a community can now be as big or as small as you want it to be—and the Internet is a big place.

Instead of listening to the brand, consumers started listening to each other. They were engaging in conversations that brands weren't part of, building their own native content, and sharing it with the masses. As the collective voice of the consumer grew stronger, brands could no longer control the conversation they once dominated. Empowered by the new information that was available to them, customers, in turn, were losing trust in brands' commitments to keeping their promises.

It was a radically recast landscape, full of challenges, for which digital transformation appeared to be the solution. Just as the digital revolution had initially blown up everything that brands had become accustomed to, now it was going to make everything much better. The idea was to use digital technologies to modify existing business processes and/or to create new ones that would change culture and customer experiences in response to changing business and market requirements. Through this process of digital transformation, brands would be in a position to achieve the maximum business benefit from the digital revolution. In short order, digital transformation became the reflex corporate response, the panacea.

Then 2008 brought the financial crisis. The total value of US stocks declined by $7.4 trillion, while economic growth slowed, and unemployment levels ballooned. Almost overnight, companies went from reporting strong growth to experiencing perilous levels of uncertainty. To survive this calamitous financial downturn, brands had to move quickly to staunch the flow of red ink, cut costs, and deliver on improved organizational efficiency. Brands were in a scramble to save themselves and digital technology was there to throw them a lifeline. It was a pivotal moment in the evolution of digital transformation as a business strategy.

Digital transformation was originally a blanket term for digital solutions that would make a business more successful. It was expected that revenue and profits would increase as a result of the deeper relationships that technology would support and foster. Businesses had high expectations that digital transformation could move their brands in any number of different directions. It would certainly help bridge the gap, created by social media, that had muted a brand's near-monopoly over communications. It would act as re-connective tissue.

But then digital transformation morphed. Following the financial downturn in 2008, brands that were struggling to survive adopted digital transformation to serve a single purpose: slash costs and increase efficiency. And as we know, the downturn didn't last just a few months or even years. The aftershocks continued to be felt well past the five-year mark; during this period, "efficiency" was elevated to become the top corporate priority, and digital transformation gained Superman status.

Where was the customer in all this? Not top-of-mind, that's for sure. By this point, the priority of delivering quality CX had been supplanted by the drive to reduce costs. CEOs became reliant on all things digital to drive innovation, and improving organizational efficiency was no longer just a means to an end—it became an end in itself. In our view, the ascendancy of technology, specifically digital transformation, was the eye of that perfect storm and the point at which brands lost perspective.

Regularly overlooked today is the fact that technology is, in essence, just a tool. Digital transformation was never going to solve *all* the issues that businesses faced at the beginning of the digital revolution. So why would it now? Technology is powerful, but it can only see the present and the past. In contrast, humans can look ahead, re-set priorities, re-evaluate benchmarks, launch initiatives and, most importantly, shift future mindsets. Unlike digital transformation, CX Transformation has a living, beating heart because it depends on leadership, management, and employees to spark, nurture, and sustain relationships with customers.

Chapter 4

Digital Transformation Meets CX Transformation

**Combine CX and digital transformation
to achieve significant ROI.**

LYFT, Uber, Purple, Casper: these are Brands that were born, quite literally, out of the post-industrial age we live in. Technology defines them; they wouldn't exist without it. In many cases, they became so quickly ingrained in our daily lives that it's hard to even call them upstarts. And yet as recently as 2017, they were just that. These new giants of the 21st century have made short work of disrupting mature markets. They challenge any, and all, who cling to traditional business models and conventional distribution channels.

One thing that these disruptor brands have in common is their unequivocal belief that the customer rules. Fueled by technology, disruptor brands are "digital natives" that have never known life before the digital revolution. They start with better logistics and a closer connection with the customer than could ever have been possible in the past. They build an integrated customer feedback loop right into their brand operations from day one. As a result, they already know their customers better than their traditional competitors simply because they're closer to them.

Disruptors are ahead of the game from the start because of their superior knowledge of their customers. Every interaction is automatically an opportunity to collect data and synthesize knowledge of their customers' needs. As a result, disruptor businesses are in a prime position to capitalize on the information they collect by turning it around and giving it back to customers in the form they want: a better experience every time they engage with the brand. In other words, combining the power of digital tools with effective CX can work magic.

Meanwhile, many mature businesses are still coming to grips with the permanent impact of the digital revolution. As they sort through the rubble, they struggle to adapt. That said, the majority of CEOs have understood from the start that the most viable response to the digital revolution would be to join the party, transform their business operations and make the most out of what digital was offering. It wasn't difficult to genuinely believe that digital transformation could open the door to higher revenue and profits.

But digital transformation hasn't turned out to be the miracle cure that was originally anticipated. Instead, it has become one of the reasons that brands get stuck. While it may have increased organizational efficiency, it hasn't done anything to differentiate one brand from the next. On the contrary, it has more frequently enabled increased competition with multiple similar products glutting the market and catalyzing unexpected outcomes—most notably, price wars.

Historically, businesses could always count on innovation to fuel growth. It was a firm foundation on which to build a brand and showcase competitive advantage. Better yet, customers were willing to pay a premium for innovative products and services. This manifested in profits, almost guaranteeing years of ongoing success. But increased accessibility to technology, and the innovation that it makes possible, has also lowered barriers to entry for upstarts into almost any given market. Innovation no longer requires scary levels of investment; it's now accessible to anyone who wants to copy, knock off, produce for less money, use inferior or less-expensive materials, or charge less for their services.

You could say that "to innovate" became synonymous with "let's drive down prices." So, while digital transformation was certainly necessary in many situations, and was a logical response to a rapidly morphing landscape, it also diminished brand differentiation. It has been the cause of an epidemic of sameness resulting in a dynamic that makes perfect sense: if you can't perceive the difference between two products, your decision rests on price. For brands striving to differentiate, this is their reality. It's a constant battle.

Now, let's circle back to the brand-customer disconnect, where we can see, amid all this clamor, how the customer's voice fades into the background. Every quarter, leadership's top priority is to show value to shareholders. Working diligently to hit benchmarks, CEOs still rely on short-term profits to demonstrate the health of the brand. But while they focus on immediate results, why are they not using digital tools to also help build deeper trust-based customer relationships? Why not deploy these same digital tools to drive long-term results, too? Wouldn't combining Digital transformation with CX Transformation efforts be a whole lot more … transformative?

+++

In 2020, COVID-19 engulfed the globe, throwing into question much of what we take for granted as a society. It also taught businesses, big and small, a harsh lesson. With entire nations under lockdown, commerce was upended and brands were even further distanced from their customers. Businesses that didn't already have digital channels and e-commerce platforms in place had to react quickly to survive. And the first survivors would be the prescient brands that had already combined their CX best practices with digital channels; they would be among those capable of transforming quickly.

What we're continuing to learn from COVID-19 also proves the point that if a brand can successfully marry its CX with its digital capabilities, it can pivot quickly, even almost overnight. The upshot: both the brand and the customer benefit. Whether it's a grocery store, a restaurant, or a gym, a business's ability to move swiftly and implement changes in its operations makes a crucial difference. Digital transformation empowers On/Off channel changes (We're open! We're not! Curbside pickup only!) while CX keeps customers up-to-date on new protocols and reassures them that they can still get their hands on the provisions and services they need—via contactless delivery, of course.

COVID-19 also brusquely exposed the weakness of businesses that depend primarily on in-person interactions. The shopping environment changed rapidly, accelerating the demise of some notable Brands. Neiman Marcus, JC Penney, and Lord & Taylor, three venerable players in the US department store sector, have all declared bankruptcy. As we're writing this book, we're watching Macy's and Saks Fifth Avenue struggle to stay afloat. Ironically, with so many retailers floundering, Macy's concern is no longer with its conventional competitors. Instead, it's facing the goliath Amazon and its superior delivery system.

"Customers today are comparing your brand to everyone, not just your competitors. Your brand's ability to deliver an easy, effortless experience is being compared to companies like Amazon and Apple," said Jerry Pasierb, Vice President, Customer Experience Strategy, PNC. In other words, it's no longer just about how your brand performs after the customer has signed on; it's as much, if not more, about their experience of acquiring your product or service in the first place!

In response to the challenges that the COVID-19 pandemic unleashed, brands scrambled to stay relevant by accelerating their digital transformation efforts. They had made the mistake of thinking they had more than enough time and, if it hadn't been for the onslaught of COVID-19, they might have. But the reality is that if a brand is already struggling to stay alive, digital transformation alone won't deliver the quick fix that they mistakenly believe will save them.

Back when businesses were first adopting digital transformation, a strong relationship between CEOs and their Chief Technology Officers seemed like a winning ticket. Together, they were highly constructive and successful in extracting efficiency from digital. They worked in sync to quickly establish plans, drive development forward, and improve organizationally in ways that saved the brand money. You would assume that this kind of effective teamwork would have yielded impressive results, not least in service of organizational efficiency.

But our research also showed that significant improvements in organizational efficiency were reported by 83% of brands that had achieved high levels of digital transformation in combination with CX Transformation. In contrast, among brands that had achieved the same levels of digital transformation, but without the accompanying CX Transformation, only 55% reported a concurrent increase in organizational efficiency for their efforts.

Turning to revenue and profits for the brands that achieved the highest level of digital transformation, 52% reported a significant increase in revenue and 43% reported a significant increase in profits for their efforts. But those that coordinated both digital and CX Transformation efforts and achieved the highest level of transformation in both areas were far more likely to report significantly increased revenue (74%) and profits (70%) for their efforts.

These results clearly show the value and importance of including CX Transformation in the process of adapting to the post-

COVID-19 economy and reawakening the importance of CX in staying successful.

Even better, combining CX and digital transformation initiatives also yields additional improvements in the areas of customer satisfaction and employee satisfaction compared to those brands that focused exclusively on digital transformation. PNC's Jerry Pasierb looks at new technology as an "enabler" for improving customer experience, rather than a solution. And he believes that having solid processes, engaged employees, and the right technology can deliver an optimal customer experience. So while it's clear to us that technology can facilitate smoother interactions which, in turn, help build trust and ultimately lead to deeper relationships, these are definitely not the only initiatives needed to be successful.

We're convinced that brands with a more acute understanding of customer experience, i.e., those that lean into CX Transformation even at the expense of digital transformation, are heading toward an epiphany. Companies with this mindset understand that listening to the customer and delivering better-quality CX can become their brand's competitive advantage, replacing price and innovation as its primary differentiator. They also understand that building better customer relationships hinges on a brand's ability to transform its own culture, too.

Deepak Sharma, Managing Director at Deloitte Consulting, expressed it so well to us:

> "Customer decision-making has undergone an 'Amazon-ification'. Customers want to compare every alternative before making a purchase. That wasn't possible before Amazon and it's affected how everyone does business."

Chapter 5

CX Transformation is Cultural Transformation

Transforming a culture takes a lot more effort, but achieves a much greater reward.

"We're leading; our brand is thriving."

"Our customers love us and trust us."

"We're confident we're consistently making the right decisions."

In a perfect world, we'd all be able to make such glory-filled claims. But here's the reality: today, most brands would need to seriously shake things up before making even one of these statements with confidence. Digital transformation let us down; it didn't live up to its marquee billing. And while brands are still perennially fixated on results and efficiency, we at ONR have seen, time and time again, that what's needed is a real culture shift. To improve customer relationships, brands have to start by looking within, checking their values and aligning their culture.

Why? Because how a brand relates to its customers is a direct reflection of how it functions internally and how it treats its own people. If there are internal issues, they will show up in the culture. As Travis Howe from The Walt Disney Company put it in a conversation with us, "*If* you want to be a client-first organization, it's more than a *doing* culture, it's a *living* culture." CX Transformation is actually about transforming people, which means that it has to be a Cultural Transformation, too.

This makes perfect sense when we consider today's business environment. We already know that technology generally, and digital transformation specifically, have struggled to deliver discernable and lasting brand value. As we discussed earlier, innovation no longer serves its masters, and no longer contributes to significant differentiation in the marketplace. Margins are thin, and so many CEOs have tunnel vision when it comes to responding to the demands of their shareholders and investors. And through their actions and strategies, brands have conditioned their customers to believe that price is all that matters. Something has to give.

To change the way a brand acts, it has to start by changing the way it thinks—how it sets strategies and makes decisions. If achieving CX Transformation is the goal, then a brand's decisions and actions, both internally and externally, must reflect its top priority, the customer. It's a mission that must also be embedded in the brand's culture. If the prevailing mindsets and attitudes within the organization don't support that collective mission, CX Transformation won't take hold, because a brand's entire culture has to shift, adapt, absorb, and embrace the change if the transformation is to succeed.

As a good starting point for a culture shift that is so obvious that it's often overlooked, we advise leaders of all sizes and types of organizations to take a hard look at their mission statement. Hopefully, it's already an authentic and practical expression of core values and vision, but does it emphasize the importance of the customer as its top priority? It should. It's the customer who deserves pride of place.

Shubha Rao, Community Operations, Head of Strategy & Planning, at Uber, wants businesses to lead from their Mission and their Vision, because it creates a strong connection with their customers and, even more importantly, connection with their employees. This translates into every interaction that they have with someone external to the company, and it doesn't have to be a customer support experience.

> "It's very easy for companies to achieve product parity with a competitor. And then it becomes about what else can you bring to the table. You're then trying to win customers' loyalty and dollars based on whether it's easy to do business with you. Because people want it to be convenient, they want it to be easy, and they want it to be effortless."

Why is this so important? Let's take a look at a re-oriented brand that has successfully aligned its actions with its mission and values. Its entire organization, including the board, is reminded regularly of why the brand exists: to serve its customers well. The better a brand treats its customers, the stronger the bond of trust between them grows; the greater the trust, the more resilient the relationship will be. And when the company mission statement spells it out clearly, customers and employees alike benefit from this precision. Alex Genov, Head of Customer Research at Zappos, suggested that culture is not just a set of rules that you create at a retreat and come back knowing you have it right. Culture is living your values.

CX Transformation is a top-down process, with the CEO as its Number One advocate. The CEO models the new thinking and sets the direction. The CEO leads the brand's re-integration of the customer into the decision-making process. And the CEO brings authenticity and intention to the initiative. As Deb Kerschen, a veteran Customer Support Manager who spent 16 years at Intel points out, a brand has to have an executive with a voice if it wants to advance a transformational agenda. Only leadership can help it do that. Otherwise, there's just a bunch of people hitting their heads against an invisible ceiling and going nowhere. Brands that value their customers' relationships communicate it credibly through their actions. So, the CEO who leads an organization committed to CX Transformation is also at the helm of a cultural transformation with the mandate to re-orient the brand from the inside out. Serving the customer becomes an organization-wide imperative.

Shifting a brand's culture to become more customer-centric requires that the brand reframe its priorities, especially in the way it moves into evaluating success against a new and different set of standards. Efficiency is no longer the only game in town; instead, the focus is on building customer knowledge. Every person in the company is educated and trained to be comfortable with embracing the concept in a way that is easy and feels natural. From the call center to the C-suite, employees and leadership alike ask themselves, "How will my actions serve to nurture and deepen the customer's relationship with our brand?" Everyone becomes fluent in the language of connection. In fact, a cultural transformation brings the entire organization and its brand back to the values that made it successful in the first place.

As the brand rallies around its customer, it also aligns around its collective goal of building trust-based relationships. As in all aspects of life, authenticity is key. Hollow promises and quick fixes can only take us so far. For example, merely initiating a policy on managing customer relationships may get traction initially, but its impact will be limited to those who interact directly with customers. Those who don't interact will come to see it as "putting lipstick on a pig" and reject it as inauthentic. Inevitably, the customer will come to the same conclusion.

The opposite is true when efforts are made with authentic intentions. When customers recognize that a brand is invested in earning and keeping their trust, the terms of the relationship change. The customer feels valued. They're no longer a number on a spreadsheet; instead, they become an active player with the power to evoke passion, empathy, concern. For employees, the customer becomes real, the customer has a voice and, most crucially, they come to realize that the customer has a choice of whether to stick with a brand or not, based, at least partially, on each employee's contribution (or lack of!) to the customer's experience of the brand. "Leadership has to create a culture that encourages the front line to really listen and be advocates for the change they see in daily interactions ... or they risk them perceiving that CX doesn't really matter," said Adam Lebofsky, Senior Vice President and Executive Director of Marketing at JPMorgan Chase.

Once you've committed to a re-orientation process, the real work begins when you launch your strategic plan and introduce CX Transformation to the people who will implement it. This is a critical moment. For this process to deliver positive results, CX Transformation must permeate your organization's culture, touching every part of it. Every member of your organization must be encouraged to become invested in its success. It's a step-by-step process, an internal attitude overhaul, a culture shift. As the leader of both the organization and of the transformation effort, a brand's CEO is heading up a mission that depends on nothing less than a full-scale team effort.

The plan also calls for the democratization of data within your organization; an initiative that makes customer knowledge available and accessible to everyone. It also calls for a company-wide program that encourages and rewards everyone for building better CX by taking actions that are informed by customer knowledge. According to Jerry Pasierb,

> "Culture is key; leadership must walk the talk with a collective focus on employee and customer experience."

As everyone adapts to this re-oriented way of doing business, they will develop a clear understanding of the brand's mission and of their individual roles in supporting it. This generates positive energy; employees will be eager to share their knowledge and greater alignment will develop between teams. The value of collaborating across the organization becomes tangible, and teams will actively seek out new opportunities to work together more efficiently to deepen customer relationships.

The outcome of this cultural shift is more than just greater efficiency; it also fosters a much higher level of engagement by all employees. CX Transformation creates an informed and transparent work environment. With increased clarity of goals and objectives, employees understand that they share a common purpose, one they perceive to be noble because it's authentic. Even better, they're aware they play an essential role in it.

+++

If all of this sounds ambitious to you, even like an insurmountable assignment, we get it, but we urge you not to back off before you even begin. Remember that all successful brands started out with a deep sense of commitment to the people they served. Employees knew it and felt it because they were the conduits. But as success grew, those same brands became distracted by other imperatives considered vital to increasing revenue and profits. Nurturing customer relationships became de-prioritized.

In contrast, when an organization re-orients internally to re-focus on the customer, it shows in its culture. Customers are drawn to brands that seek to deepen their connections and honor their relationships, and to organizations made up of individuals whose mission is to treat customers well and make them feel seen and heard.

So when a CEO poses the question: "Do we have what we need to help our brand create deeper customer relationships?" they should really be asking themselves, "Do we know our customers well enough to make the best decisions on their behalf?", "Does our brand culture nurture customer relationships?" and "How authentic are we?"

Breathing new life into the brand-customer relationship is achievable as long as it's understood that CX Transformation starts from the inside. CX Transformation is, after all, also Cultural Transformation.

Chapter 6

When Data is Like Gold

You must know your customer. There are no shortcuts.

It starts with the customer. As Blake Morgan, CX Futurist and the author of *The Customer of the Future,* told us,

> "Too often, leaders are concerned about the bottom line instead of customers. Investing in CX requires putting forth time, effort, and resources, and many leaders are hesitant to put money towards something that they don't think proves an obvious return. In these cases, customer experiences never improve. But in reality, investing in customer experience pays off in increased revenue, customer loyalty and a host of other factors.

To overcome this challenge, employees need to tie CX to bottom-line growth to get leaders on their side."

Customers are a brand's lifeblood. The world's most successful Brands, such as, Apple, Costco, Domino's, and Starbucks, engage their customers early and often. They are consistent. They never stop building relationships with every one of their customers. They expect to connect with them on an emotional level at every interaction. And they know that strong, trust-based customer relationships will result in the best possible CX.

A smart brand commits to doing its best for its customers for the long term. But what the smartest brands also know is that good CX brings added value. CX Transformation addresses the core internal problem that brands face today—differentiation—not just its external symptom, stagnant financial results. In 2021, a customer whose experience with a brand is consistently good is now a brand's most powerful differentiator.

The emotional connection makes the difference. It's what distinguishes a real relationship from a mere transaction. It's like Tinder vs Match in the dating site world. If you're competing with other brands strictly on price, chasing transactions rather than customers, that's the Tinder model. If you're looking to build long-term relationships with customers in hopes of securing their "forever" commitment to your brand, you're in the Match world. Either way, the customer is the priority and improving the relationship is the mission.

At ONR, we've advised brands for years on CX Transformation, helping them to strengthen their customer relationships by improving their customer knowledge. We regularly see brands that have the potential to deepen their connections with customers, if only they would measure their interactions better. But the metrics they use to collect customer data are often ill-conceived; their focus is limited to measuring a customer's feelings in the moment, rather than the depth of their relationship with the brand as it builds.

If the customer knowledge that a brand collects is weak, then it's left guessing and making assumptions about who it's in a relationship with. To improve the relationship, you have to know your customer first. There are no shortcuts. Listen to Alex Genov, Head of Customer Research at Zappos:

> "Customers are not data, they are people ... we cannot average human experience."

Customer data is worth nothing if it doesn't tell a story. But when it does, it's like gold. Smart brands excel at working both efficiently and effectively with the data they collect. They piece together a narrative that tells the story of why and how their customers make the decisions they make. This gives them a window into their customers' mindsets and tastes; they know how they're reacting, whether it's with pleasure or frustration. These brands are fully in tune with their customers' wants, needs, and desires.

Once a brand learns how to use its customer knowledge to maximum advantage, it's like inviting the customer to take a seat at the boardroom table. Through the data that the brand has collected, customers tell the brand's leadership their stories, and contribute to the discussion, while the leaders themselves gain knowledge and understanding, clarity and detail.

To build this level of deep reciprocity into the brand-customer relationship, leaders need to understand what actually matters to a customer. And *that* is the value of customer data. The answers are all there, data is the linchpin.

Now, while there are brands that don't yet know how to get the most out of the data that they collect, they can change that through CX Transformation. Brands can realize the value and potential inherent in customer knowledge. By incorporating customer data into the brand's decision-making process, it becomes possible for everyone, organization-wide, to take actions that both prioritize the customer and feed the bottom line. Time after time, we see results that include increased revenue, higher profits, improved organizational efficiency, and better employee performance.

At ONR, we've developed a systematic approach to CX Transformation, which we are sharing with you in this book. In Part I, we laid out for you the insights and strategies that deal with the realities of the world today.

In Part III, we'll open up our playbook for you to explain in detail, step-by-step, how to turn CX data into CX knowledge. What you have there is our advice and counsel on how you can restore the emotional connection between your customer and your brand, strengthen the bond between your data and your brand's decisions and actions, and build a healthy, long-term relationship between your Customers' Experience and your brand's revenues and profits.

Next, in Part IV, where you'll benefit from the insights of experts with real-world experience in CX Transformation, we'll show you some examples of what happens when plans become action.

In Part V, the author shares his own experiences of helping clients implement CX Transformation successfully, together with some advice on how to maintain momentum and engagement.

In Part VI, we provide a guide to tracking your progress along the Steps involved in successfully implementing CX Transformation.

At the end of the book, we've provided an extensive summary of ONR's own research of some 1,000 carefully selected brands over a wide range of businesses and industries. It shows conclusively that brands reaching the highest level of CX Transformation have achieved amazing levels of revenues, profits, and organizational efficiency when compared to similar brands in their field that are at the lowest level of CX Transformation.

For some brands, CX Transformation provides an escape route from the downward spiral of declining profits. For others, it is quite simply the pathway home, a return to the core principles and honest values that defined their original mission. Most important though, CX Transformation is the solution for

CEOs who are intent on increasing the velocity of their CX Transformation efforts.

And trust us, it works!

PART III

Transforming Customer Data into Gold: The CX Transformation Playbook

It's time to get to work!

In the following pages, we'll take you through our systematic approach to CX Transformation. Our objective is to pass along our deep knowledge and accumulated experience so that you'll be able to absorb and embrace it within your own brand's culture. This is not theoretical, it's a Playbook for you and your organization to follow, Level by Level, Step by Step.

Fundamental to our approach is the "Collect/Share/Act" formula that we've developed through many years of helping clients implement CX Transformation and achieve significant paybacks. It may sound simple—*Collect the right data; Share it across all teams; Act on it*—yet it's hugely empowering. You will embed Collect/Share/Act into your C-suite's mindset from Day One, then you'll introduce it incrementally, department-by-department and. eventually, you will roll it out company-wide.

Chapter 7

Introduction: Collect/Share/Act

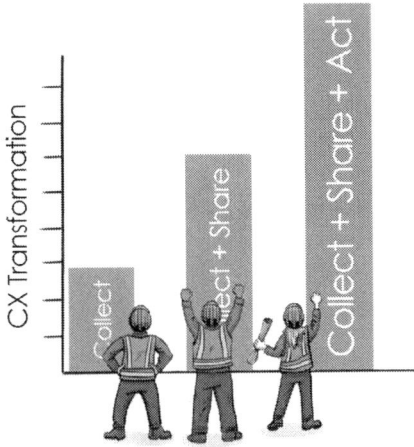

Leaders, let Collect/Share/Act guide you; make it your mantra. As you progress through the Levels, return to it often and in time you'll be able to quantify its transformative effect. Your people will start contributing to continuous and ongoing improvements, rather than remaining enslaved by inefficient, one-time fixes. Subscribe to the Collect/Share/Act formula and you'll see how your CX data will transform into valuable knowledge, deeper customer relationships, improved customer experience, and better organizational efficiency, all of which are the essential contributors to the resulting increased revenues and profits.

COLLECT the *right* data.

To know your customer better, you have to invest time in gathering information and building stores of customer knowledge. The most effective way to do this is to gather customer feedback across all key points of customer interactions. Many brands have illusions about the efficacy of their data collection practices; they think they're already doing a good job. "We have more information about our customers than any of our competitors," they might say. In some cases, this may be true, but has it delivered a positive payoff? Probably not. The solution is quite simple: *Collect better data*!

SHARE the data with everyone.

Some brands commit substantial resources to collecting and interpreting data and coming up with significant insights and knowledge, only to sit on it and do nothing with it. Sharing knowledge and insight right across the organization is what's really needed to deepen customer relationships. There are many reasons why CX data isn't currently being shared optimally across your organization. A key one is the existence of those darned departmental silos; their leaders are reluctant to share information beyond their own departments. That's such a waste! You need to create an environment that makes customer knowledge accessible, and then *Share it!*

ACT on the data.

Organization-wide, all teams should be applying customer knowledge to their planning, decisions, and actions. Team by team, department by department, a brand will transform when the entire organization aligns its decision-making process and takes action in service of the customer. With deeper customer relationships comes the potential for increased revenue and profits. So don't only advocate, but be committed to the principle of *Act for the customer*.

Chapter 8

Level 1: Plan

Level 1 Playbook Steps Summary

1. Align Mission Statement with CX Values

2. Map it out

3. Manage expectations

4. Assign a CX Transformation Point Person

5. Embed Collect/Share/Act

6. Establish CX-specific KPIs

At Level 1, your mandate is to lay the groundwork for successful CX Transformation. This is where many brands sit today and your brand may be here as well. As you go through the Steps outlined below, you'll discover that this involves setting benchmarks and expectations, aligning goals, milestones, and language, embedding the Collect/Share/Act formula, and establishing CX-specific Key Performance Indicators (KPIs).

Planning for Level 1 starts in your C-suite. To succeed with CX Transformation, strong leadership is not just desirable, it's mandatory. As the CEO, it's your role to ensure that the CX Transformation process is fully understood by your entire Leadership Team. The starting point is explaining its goals in the clearest terms: namely, to deepen customer relationships, to improve all employees' customer knowledge, and to reap the benefits in terms of increased revenues and profits.

While the CEO is by far the best person to lead the CX Transformation initiative and ensure transparency, every member of the C-suite has a role to play. Full engagement is essential as you develop a comprehensive strategic plan and begin to prepare your organization's culture for implementing CX Transformation. Most importantly, your own powers of inspiration and persuasion will be called on to drive the mission to success.

Level 1 Playbook Steps

Step 1—Align Your Mission Statement with CX Values

Start by reviewing your Mission Statement. While it may not normally be top-of-mind for you and your team, we think it should be. Situations differ, of course, as does the value placed on such corporate credos. At some companies, the Mission Statement is nothing more than a few benign lines in an annual report. At others, it's an earnest and literal expression of an organization's vision and values. We're all for the latter, because we believe that a clear Mission Statement is a potent tool in the hands of a strong leader who is looking to re-energize teams and communicate vision and values. And, to be completely open, it's essential for implementing CX Transformation successfully.

The purpose of Step 1 is to establish the primacy of the customer in your organization's priorities. Your Mission Statement should be clear that your primary objective is to deepen your relationship with your customers. This may sound simplistic, but it's important that leadership assesses proposed decisions and actions against the stated mission. It will prove to be a powerful resource, one that you'll call upon again and again to keep the brand focused and to drive appropriate actions, convince others to take risks, and implement quick corrective actions when called for. It will also prove useful when you're faced with pushback or questions. It's your North Star, guiding your CX Transformation initiative and keeping your organization on track and moving in the right direction.

So, Step 1 requires that you dust off that Mission Statement and re-assess it through the fresh eyes of CX Transformation. Ask yourself if it stands up in today's environment, is still relevant, and is on point. Most important, don't just accept it at face value; urge your team to critique it and identify what's missing. Does satisfying your customers' wants, needs and desires come through loud and clear? If not, your Mission Statement needs to be updated.

Step 2—Map It Out

This Playbook maps out the CX Transformation process for you. Follow the Steps at each Level and you'll reach your destination. Since every organization is different, we advise you to break it down into micro-steps, if necessary, to make it feel more manageable. Define key milestones so that your leadership can visualize what success will look like and how the five Levels build on each other to eventually deliver the transformation that you need. By mapping out your organization's unique short- and long-term milestones, your leadership will be so much better equipped to understand the areas of customer experience that are relevant to your purpose; this will help increase the velocity of CX Transformation right out of the gate.

Step 3—Manage Expectations

Your leadership must establish realistic expectations about ROI opportunities and limitations at the early Levels of CX Transformation. The process succeeds through a methodical approach, accompanied with steady ROI. By the same token, just as you should manage financial investments prudently and resist the urge to over-invest at this early stage. CX Transformation is not a one-inning game; as your brand graduates to each new Level, the likelihood of achieving significant ROI beyond just revenue and profits will become ever more apparent: first, in terms of customer satisfaction, next, in employee satisfaction, and finally, in organizational efficiency. In short, you, the CEO, must communicate the message of avoiding unrealistic expectations of early ROI clearly to your C-suite, and beyond.

Step 4—Assign a CX Transformation Point Person

While every member of your C-suite has a role to play in this process, assigning a dedicated point person can be very powerful; we've found that it usually increases the effectiveness of CX Transformation by a large margin. In many cases, we've seen brands add their CXO or CCO to the C-suite to head up their CX Transformations. This is, of course, a decision that ultimately depends on the size of your organization and the confidence of its leadership. Our view is that while beefing up the C-suite in this way may not seem to be as important in the early days, it will become more so as you work through the Levels and expand your CX Transformation. If you feel that rallying your C-suite under the CX Transformation banner will be challenging for you to lead yourself, then a point person will definitely be helpful, but no matter how you do it, you must make sure that your CX Transformation leader has direct access to their CEO.

Step 5—Embed Collect/Share/Act

As we discussed in the Introduction to this Playbook, "Collect/Share/Act" is the formula we've developed for achieving CX Transformation. It's short for *Collect the right data/Share it across all teams/Act on it.*

Start embedding the **Collect/Share/Act** mantra into your C-suite's mindset. This is how you use your CX data to improve customer experience and deepen customer relationship so that you can achieve those increased revenues and profits. Collect/Share/Act is an integral part of ensuring that your brand stays focused on the achievements at each Level that help it progress to the next Level with an efficiency that will become the hallmark of your CX Transformation program.

Step 6—Establish CX-specific Key Performance Indicators

It is absolutely critical that you establish the appropriate KPIs for your CX Transformation program. You'll want to get this right. So much depends on accurately defining what your brand's focus should be in terms of data. We've seen too many brands spend an inordinate amount of time and effort collecting too much of what they don't need and not enough of what they could really use. That's a huge waste. What you *do* need is data that will most effectively measure your progress towards your own customer experience goals.

And never forget that since what matters most to your brand are revenue and profits, then as you work your way through the five Levels, these two metrics will be more and more closely connected to your CX Transformation efforts.

You may have heard some CX evangelists preach, "Don't worry about measuring hard metrics, this is about feelings." Wrong! Sales and revenue are the *most* important metrics. Without them, there is no brand. However, at this early stage, the KPIs that matter are those that measure both your customers' trust in your brand and your employees' trust in your brand. These metrics should be tracked and shared regularly within your C-suite. Pay specific attention to where your CX Transformation efforts are taking place, and monitor these key metrics closely across those specific departments. Set your KPIs to help you understand how CX Transformation efforts are progressing both internally and externally. As CX Transformation efforts progress, you will want to investigate how your KPIs directly influence your revenue and profits.

Chapter 9
Level 2: Learn

Level 2 Playbook Steps Summary

1. CoRE Team

2. CoRE Team's mission

3. Customer priorities for post-sales support

4. Mind the gaps

5. KPIs for post-sales support

Once your C-suite is aligned and focused on launching your CX Transformation, you can begin to turn abstraction into action. At Level 2, you'll designate the post-sales support (or post-sales departments) as the launching pad for CX Transformation efforts. Now you'll be building the team that will actually drive CX Transformation. You'll activate operational improvements using C/S/A. Essentially, Level 2 lays the foundations for current and future CX Transformation efforts.

Post-sales is usually where you'll find a critical mass of people who already interact with customers more frequently than anyone else in the organization. They're the ones on the other end of the phone 24/7, and/or otherwise communicating with your customers, day-in, day-out. This is where we advise you to start.

Of course, not everyone in your organization thinks the same way as you. You may be asked why Sales or Marketing isn't the starting point. In our experience, we've found that the post-sales team is the one most likely to have already started developing a CX mindset simply by osmosis. These people are already immersed in a regular stream of customer feedback, and they're more attuned to their needs, which makes them the most likely advocates for your customers, which is precisely what you need at the start of your CX Transformation initiative.

Level 2 Steps

Step 1—Build your CoRE Team

The CoRE Team (*Customer Relationships are Everything*) will direct your CX Transformation efforts. This team's members are the pioneers who will take the lead in teaching all departments how to Collect/Share/Act. They're ultimately accountable for the success of your CX Transformation efforts and will report directly to you, the CEO, through their Team Leader.

The right composition of your CoRE Team is vitally important. It needs a strong leader who has your ear. This leader should understand the importance of developing deep sustaining customer relationships and be a passionate advocate for your customers. In addition, and possibly most importantly, this leader needs to be able to speak the financial language of the boardroom.

The CoRE Team should start small, with just a few members who will initially be working with just one department. Strongly consider selecting these early team members from your post-sales department, since they already have built-in knowledge of how post-sales works. This will help your CoRE Team establish credibility quickly. Note that these team members must be detached from their post-sales function so that they can work full-time on the CX Transformation initiative.

Your CoRE Team should meet regularly with your C-suite to report on its progress. As CX Transformation accelerates, and your brand reaches deeper levels of relationship with your customers, this team should be introduced to your board to report on the progress of your CX Transformation program, so make sure you choose a leader who can establish rapport with your board members.

Step 2—Establish Your CoRE Team's Mission

The key priority for your CoRE Team is to educate post-sales staff about the ROI that CX Transformation will deliver, and how your brand will achieve the consequent benefits by optimizing how that department collects CX data, shares CX data and acts on CX data. This will empower your post-sales function with the customer knowledge necessary to effectively prioritize the actions that it must take to deepen relationships with your customers.

Step 3—Develop a List of Customer Priorities for Post-sales Support

The ongoing engagement between your CoRE Team and post-sales will be focused on developing key customer priorities for post-sales. This may sound simple enough, but you have to start with a deep investigation of your customers' relationship with post-sales before these priorities can be properly defined.

Your CoRE Team's first task, then, is to locate all existing customer feedback data and determine where post-sales is performing well and where they are under-performing in your customers' eyes.

Their second task is to cross-reference the list of priorities, as outlined by these customers, with the current list of post-sales business priorities, and then determine where these two lists align and where they differ. Then re-organize the post-sales priorities to more closely reflect your customers' priorities.

Their third task is to help post-sales gather additional internal customer knowledge from internal sources to ensure that the new priorities will be fully aligned with the best available information on your customers' wants, needs, and desires.

Step 4—Mind the Gaps

As your CoRE Team begins to work with post-sales, they will discover gaps that need to be closed. They need to document and categorize them as "Collecting gaps," "Sharing gaps," or "Acting gaps." Be aware that the team will be tempted to fix these gaps as they arise, but they should generally resist these urges, because these "fixes" can easily become distractions that take them down rabbit holes and prevent them from focusing on their real mission.

Even if your CoRE Team does find some glaring and easily fixable gaps within post-sales, have them focus only on sharing or acting gaps. Save the collecting gaps for Level 3 where they will inevitably encounter more gaps as they expand their efforts to include pre-sales. They will find that many of the gaps they identified at Level 2 can be solved more holistically at Level 3.

Step 5—Establish Post-sales Support Specific KPIs

As we mentioned earlier, the KPIs that matter for the CX Transformation initiative are those that measure your customer's trust in your brand and your employees' trust in your brand. These metrics should be tracked and shared regularly within the C-suite to provide visibility of the key outcomes of CX Transformation efforts.

The post-sales team may already have a set of customer-related KPIs in place, such as customer satisfaction, customer effort, or even customer loyalty. These metrics need to be shared with your CoRE Team so they, in turn, can share them regularly with the C-suite. If no metrics currently exist that capture customer experience, then your CoRE Team needs to help post-sales establish customer-related KPIs that capture this feedback.

The same holds true for employee metrics. If metrics such as employee satisfaction are already being measured, then your CoRE Team must have access to these metrics and begin sharing them regularly with the C-suite. If no employee performance metrics exist, then your CoRE Team needs to work with your HR department to establish and then track relevant metrics so that they can share them with your C-suite.

Chapter 10

Level 3: Expand

Level 3 Playbook Steps Summary

1. Expand your CoRE Team

2. Ignite collaboration

3. Optimize, using Collect/Share/Act

4. Focus on quality over quantity

5. Track employee CX decisions and actions

Now it's time to expand CX Transformation to pre-sales departments: Sales and Marketing. In a nutshell, the pre-sales' mission is to encourage customers to purchase, re-purchase and share their experience of the brand with others. In CX terms, these are your brand's efforts to persuade and influence your customers while increasing customers' trust that your brand will do right by them.

Together, pre-sales and post-sales should have all the key points of the brand-customer interaction covered. And by the time you complete Level 3, your brand will have a significantly deeper knowledge of your customers.

As you move through the Steps of Level 3, you'll see the positive effect of increasing the parameters of the transformation process. It will begin to change the way departments work together and will facilitate the way that CX Transformation actions are adopted.

Of course, customers aren't automatons, nor are they necessarily rational decision-makers. They take cognitive shortcuts, they make choices, then rationalize them afterward, which is why the world's most successful brands know how to appeal to their customers' emotions and to engage with them in ways that delight them and build trust in the brand. An emotional connection is the foundation of a deep customer relationship.

Level 3 Steps

Step 1—Expand Your CoRE Team

It's now time to expand the mission of your CoRE Team to include educating both pre- and post-sales departments about the ROI that CX Transformation will deliver and how the brand will achieve these benefits by optimizing the way that these departments *Collect* CX data, *Share* their CX data, and *Act* on their CX data.

To accomplish this expanded mission, you will need to expand your CoRE Team. We urge you to identify new members who already work in pre-sales because of their built-in knowledge of how pre-sales works. This will help your expanded CoRE Team quickly establish internal trust among members of the pre-sales functions. Look for people who understand the importance of developing deep sustaining customer relationships and have a passion for advocating for your customers.

This expanded CoRE Team will use their previous learnings from Level 2 to help drive the following actions within pre-sales in Level 3.

- Accumulate all customer feedback and determine where pre-sales is performing well and where they are under-performing in the eyes of your customers.
- Cross-reference the list of priorities as outlined by your customers with the current list of pre-sales business priorities, as well as with post-sales priorities, and determine where these three lists align and where they differ. Then re-organize the pre-sales business priorities to more closely reflect your customers' priorities.

- Help pre-sales gather additional customer knowledge from internal sources to ensure that these new top priorities will align with your customers' wants, needs and desires.
- Continue to expand the list of gaps identified in Level 2 as you work through this process with pre-sales, and continue to categorize into Collect, Share, or Act.

KPIs are key and it's important to expand the KPI collection to pre-sales, while aligning customer and employee performance metrics across these functional areas, making sure that they are shared regularly with the C-suite.

Step 2—Ignite Collaboration

Step 2 is about encouraging collaboration between your brand's post- and pre-sales departments and activate holistic thinking. A good place to start this collaboration is around common business priorities. Comparing the re-aligned pre-sales business priorities with post-sales business priorities will enable the CoRE Team to identify common problems that can be effectively resolved through collaboration. After all, your customers face similar types of issues across the multiple interaction points that involve pre- and post-sales. You'll discover that most of your common problems can be resolved when these departments work collaboratively.

Although the pre-sales folks are often characterized as "independent thinkers," with a mindset of "we know best," it's your CoRE Team's responsibility to ensure that these departments embrace CX knowledge-sharing and collaboration when addressing overlapping business priorities. Your CoRE Team must make sure that no single department is ever seen as having a greater influence than any other. All departments must collaborate as peers, with your CoRE Team playing the role of referee when necessary. The outcomes of increased collaboration will include improved efficiency and cost reduction, which will help ensure that collaboration between these departments becomes a new standard.

Step 3—Optimize using Collect/Share/Act

One of the key areas of collaboration will be to align and optimize data collection processes to ensure that your brand is collecting the *right* CX data to influence decision-making around your key business priorities. Your CoRE Team must take the lead in aligning the CX data collection activities from all interaction points with the business priorities of pre- and post-sales. This ensures that you are capturing the CX data that will guide your brand's decisions and actions. Re-examine the key data collection gaps that you identified at Level 2 and are now building on at Level 3. Do your best to close at least some of these gaps at this point.

As you are optimizing data collection, you must do the same for CX data sharing. Your CoRE Team needs to identify the internal employees who need each data point being collected and ensure that they have regular access to this data to drive their decisions and actions, regardless of who "owns" the data and where the data was collected.

Step 4—Focus on Quality Over Quantity

Now it's time to assess and optimize all your data collection methodologies to ensure that they are now delivering the best response rates possible, along with the most reliable and meaningful customer experience information.

The common complaint often voiced by employees from many departments, and often used as an excuse for a lack of effective action is, "We need more data." The fact is that brands today have more data than they have ever had before. What employees are really saying (whether they're aware of it or not) is "We need better quality data so we can feel more confident about the decisions we're making."

Here's how your CoRE Team can help with this process. We find that the first common issue around optimizing data collection is about how the data is collected. We're sure that you've noticed how "other brands" tend to use obnoxious and pestering methods to solicit feedback from their customers. 'Take my survey, take my survey!' Then they often focus on collecting more data points, again and again, from the same customer across the same customer interaction. At every interaction there is a website invitation, an email invitation, and/or a text message invitation. "Rate our brand, rate our brand, rate our brand." This approach is both intrusive and annoying and, because it's short-sighted and ineffective, it often undermines a brand's effort to build deeper customer relationships.

So *your* CoRE Team should look for any of these practices that have crept into your own brand's data collection practices, and eliminate them immediately. Whenever sales agents insist that customers rate them 5 out of 5, it creates a bias in responses and undermines the quality of the data collected. Instead, focus on improving the quality of the feedback that you're getting by taking actions that will help improve response rates and complete rates. This results in better-quality data that will lead to better analysis and more precise customer knowledge.

Step 5—Track Employee CX Decisions & Actions

An important element of CX Transformation is documenting, tracking, and reporting the key learnings. At Level 3, your CoRE Team must be tasked with setting up systems that:

- Track the decisions and actions that have been influenced by CX Knowledge,
- Identify the source(s) of the CX Knowledge that prompted the associated decision or action,
- Measure the outcomes of the decisions and actions on customer relationships.

At this point, it's OK for it to be a relatively rudimentary and highly manual process, but it can be an effective learning tool to highlight success. What you're looking to document and understand is what worked, what didn't work, why it worked, and what could be improved in the future. Only then is it worth committing resources to automate a process that has been proven to work.

As you progress further along in the CX Transformation process, you'll notice a growing appetite for this type of knowledge. Again, it's the responsibility of your CoRE Team to document and share this knowledge across the organization. Eventually, this will become one of the most vital areas of knowledge that your brand possesses, because it helps everyone anticipate actions and avoid pitfalls. Your tracking system and the way the data is archived and shared will also help prevent valuable knowledge from being lost when employees change roles or even leave your organization (and one of the natural benefits of CX Transformation is, of course, a significant reduction in those occurrences).

Chapter 11

Level 4: Advance

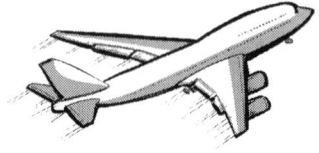

Level 4 Playbook Steps Summary

1. Expand your CoRE Team (again!)

2. Engage IT

3. Democratize your CX Data

4. Tracking Module for Employee CX decisions and actions

Level 4 is the tipping point in your brand's CX Transformation process. All the work you've done up to this point has been in preparation for what lies ahead. You've laid the groundwork, embedded core behaviors, catalyzed a cultural shift, built viable systems—all designed to make your organization more customer-centric.

As you've moved through this process, you've had a singular objective: to deepen your customer relationships and improve your brand's customer knowledge. Nothing should have distracted you from this foundational effort. Now it's time to get more sophisticated. It's time to invest in technology to facilitate the integration of the entire organization into the process. It's time to align your digital transformation and CX Transformation efforts. You're ready to flip the switch that accelerates CX Transformation.

Level 4 Steps

Step 1—Expand Your CoRE Team (again)

You start Level 4 by expanding the mission of your CoRE Team to include educating all departments about the ROI that CX

Transformation will deliver and how your brand will achieve these benefits by significantly improving the way these departments *Collect* CX data, *Share* CX data, and *Act* on CX data.

It's time to identify and assign team members from other strategic departments, including R&D and IT. As before, search out personnel who understand the importance of developing deep, sustaining customer relationships and who also have a passion for advocating for the customer.

Your CoRE Team will use what they learned during Levels 2 and 3 to help drive the following actions across all remaining departments during Level 4.

- Identify each department's priorities and cross-reference them with the list of priorities that are revealed in the data that they have collected from your customers. Use these priorities to help re-align each department's business priorities.
- Gather additional internal customer knowledge to ensure that the new top priorities will be exercised in a manner that will align with your customers' known wants, needs, and desires.
- Continue to expand the list of gaps identified with each department and make sure that they are categorized as collect, share, or act.
- KPIs are key, so it's important to establish workforce performance metrics across these departments, and make sure they are shared regularly with the C-suite.
- Identify the current customer performance metrics that each department influences, and ensure that these metrics are also regularly shared with every other department.

Step 2—Engage IT

Now, (and only now!), is the right time to engage your IT department to help your CoRE Team develop comprehensive solutions that support your CX Transformation efforts. If, for any reason, that's not something that they can undertake at this time, it's fine to acquire these solutions externally.

An example of this would be ONR's BESPOKEcx™ Solution, which helps brands identify points of interaction between their brand and their customers that are ruptured. It helps diagnose the reason for the rupture so that the right actions that repair relationships and deepen trust are finally determined. Whatever solution route you choose or build, it should focus on achieving these outcomes.

One important function of this solution will be to centrally house all of your CX data. Right now, you're probably collecting CX data using several different tools and vendors, and storing it in a variety of locations. We're not telling you to replace these other important tools and vendors. You simply ask these tools and vendors to migrate a copy of their data to your new centralized repository. You're doing this to remove barriers to acquiring and sharing CX knowledge across the organization.

All of your accumulated customer knowledge will now be integrated, absorbed, and made shareable on this central platform. And the particular magic of it will be that everyone in every department across your organization will have equal access to this customer data and will be able to transform it into customer knowledge that can be acted on.

Here are a few guidelines to help you build your data repository:

- Resist cutting corners; do not sacrifice functionality for short-term cost savings. Up to this point of the CX Transformation process, the financial investment has been low. Now it's not just desirable, it's plain imperative that you get it right.

- Most organizations think in terms of "ingestion first, connection later" i.e., "Let's collect data and store it in our 'data lake'." We'll look for ways to connect it with other data sources when we have time!" At ONR, we believe knowing exactly how data from different sources will be connected before ingesting it is a much more effective approach than trying to connect data after ingestion. Also, think about other data, such as behavioral and attitudinal, and how it can be connected, before you collect and ingest it, and take this approach whenever possible.

- The goal for everyone across your organization is to be able to easily access all of the knowledge that you have of your customers. For every piece of data that is ingested there should be a plan around who will use it, and how and, most importantly, how can it be easily accessed by your employees to be analyzed.

- Avoid building one-size-fits-all front-end dashboards; this approach seldom works because each department uses different data and applies it differently based on their specific needs. So building a one-size-fits-all front-end solution generally results in low usage, which can have a devastating impact on this investment and CX Trans-formation efforts overall.

Step 3—Democratize Your CX Data

This Step is about making it easy to share CX data across the organization so that all employees, regardless of their role, can access the customer knowledge they need. Fostering a collaborative working relationship, department-by-department, is key. As your CoRE Team leads the process, they're also helping to establish a blueprint that enables departments to build these access points for themselves.

Your CoRE Team will help departments design self-service dashboards to deliver CX data. This is not a one-size-fits-all solution. Rather, they should be designed to deliver exactly the information that each department needs in a format they require. The more a department is involved in this process, the more likely they will be invested in using the dashboards. And the more frequently the dashboards are accessed, the more valuable they become.

It's important to create awareness throughout the workforce of how the careless action (or inaction) of just one employee during a customer interaction can risk all of the work that has gone into building a relationship with that customer.

Step 4—Build a Tracking Module for Employee CX Decisions & Actions

It's time to automate your Employee CX Decision & Actions Tracking System to make it easier to track the impact of CX-driven actions.

At the previous Level, your CoRE Team was tasked with setting up a system that:

- Tracks decisions and actions influenced by CX Knowledge;
- Identifies the source of the CX Knowledge that prompted associated decisions and actions;
- Measures the outcome of the decision or action on customer relationships.

Now it's time to apply these learnings to build an automated solution that tracks CX decisions and actions.

The benefits of this should be quite clear: It will help your brand understand how customer knowledge is being applied and track the success that it's delivering. Departments will be able to measure the use of CX knowledge to inform decisions and actions. Employees will be recognized and rewarded for their CX-related initiatives and actions. Finally, the entire organization will have a set of success stories to share about how CX Transformation has delivered higher revenue and profits, increased customer and employee satisfaction, and improved organizational efficiency.

Chapter 12
Level 5: Lead

Ah, Level 5—you're finally here! You've accumulated a wealth of customer knowledge, you've shared it far and wide with your employees, and they're integrating it into your brand's decisions and actions at an unprecedented rate.

Level 5 is a different beast—it's no longer prescriptive. Armed with customer knowledge, your brand is now equipped to make informed choices and prioritize the right actions.

It's now time to choose the best path forward that will maintain and grow your brand's position in the marketplace. Taking the right actions at Level 5 will further entrench in your customers' hearts and minds that *they* are the brand's priority ahead of all other considerations. At the same time, the combination of actions that you choose will further position your brand for present and future success.

As your brand moved through the Levels of CX Transformation, some of the new choices and opportunities available will have appeared.

For some B2B brands, one important choice is whether or not to throw off the shackles of the antiquated channel-selling model and go directly to the customer. The reason this choice will have made it to the table is because of the deep understanding you've developed through your CX Transformation efforts of your customers' wants, needs, and desires.

For those of you who may be thinking of increasing the influence of your brand's digital footprint, you may want to re-think your approach and focus on delivering a mobile-first experience, so that it's always possible for your customers to connect with your brand, regardless of where and when they need to.

As part of this effort, you should also consider smoothing out the bumps that occur when customers have to switch channels during an interaction. This is important because it's often a disruption that undermines the customer's relationship with your brand. Part and parcel of this process is keeping a keen eye on emerging technologies. Integrating them into your existing technology stack can provide your customers with an improved experience and give your employees greater customer knowledge, as well as better direction on deepening customer relationships.

Another ongoing initiative is focusing on improving your internal system of measuring, identifying, and rewarding employees who make notable progress in deepening customer relationships. If your brand glossed over this Step at earlier Levels, you'll likely want to re-visit this process. There's value in ensuring that even the efforts and contributions of employees who do not interact with customers daily are effectively measured. This is not always easy to do, but if you do it properly, it will result in a more motivated workforce.

The customers who spend the most with your brand should always be top-of-mind; by the time you reach Level 5 you'll have more knowledge of this group than ever before. This is a good time to examine how you encourage these customers to continue deepening their bond with the brand. Are you just rewarding them with "free stuff," or are they receiving tangible benefits that are genuinely desired and valued? The purpose of rewards is not only to encourage your best customers to continue to deepen the relationship, but also to motivate other customers because they perceive meaningful value in staying committed to your brand.

You may find opportunities to expand the scope of the data you are collecting, and thereby inform a wider set of decisions. For example, you may be thinking about how to acquire data to help improve the accuracy of your causal analysis of your sales. Along those lines, you may also want to improve your procurement strategy. To accomplish this, you will want to start integrating more transactional, industry or even econometrics data into your data repository to help with these priorities; in other words, become even more proactive and less reactive.

You may even see a need to improve your real-time customer communication strategy. Better yet, you may have realized the value of using customer data to help with product development efforts. This is where increasing the quantity of customer demographic data, expanding the collection of attitudinal data to all customer touchpoints, and making it easier for non-technical employees to understand behavioral data will deliver meaningful payoffs and will help address these priorities.

Last, but by no means least, you may find that your current set of KPIs that measure your relationship with customers can be expanded or modified to reflect performance more accurately and drive better actions.

While all of the success that you have achieved so far has widened the gap between your brand and others, you'll continue to face challenges again and again. These include:

- Ensuring data privacy
- Upgrading legacy systems
- Experiencing a lack of resources, such as talent, knowledge, skillset, and capacity

How you prioritize and address these challenges will depend on the choices you make in response to the considerations that we detailed earlier in this Chapter.

As you can see, Level 5 is not a point of graduation, nor is it a contest you've won; it's actually part of an ongoing experience. It's a commencement, a place of choice and prioritization, a time to keep looking internally, identifying those gaps and determining the courses of action you'll take to close these gaps. In this sense, Level 5 is truly bespoke, because what your brand prioritizes to maintain its position of strength is always based on its unique market position and needs.

At Level 5, your brand has found its groove, but you still need to stay vigilant to defend its position and take advantage of the opportunities presented by the ever-changing marketplace. Make no mistake, you will always be in a continuous battle to maintain your dominant position. The difference is that at Level 5, you are facing these challenges from a position of knowledge. There's less guesswork; your decisions are so much better informed and will yield positive outcomes. Now, more than ever before, your brand is better prepared to tackle unpredictable times.

The actions you choose to take at Level 5 will evolve as both your brand and the marketplace evolves. But balance is key: don't hyper-focus on any one area and neglect others for too long. It's only by balancing your CX Transformation efforts that your brand will be optimally positioned to maintain and deepen customer relationships in this ever-changing world

The challenge will always be the same: prioritization. At Level 1, you lacked the customer knowledge required to effectively prioritize actions that would yield results. By Level 5, you're fully equipped because you have re-oriented your brand. You now have the customer knowledge to be able to effectively prioritize actions based on your customers' wants, needs, and desires, ensuring that your brand's decision-making process will lead to greater revenue and profits.

PART IV

Stories of Real-world CX Transformation Success

When your top priority is helping brands improve performance, discussing relationships is fundamental. There will be many conversations between colleagues and peers, clients and consultants, on how to improve customer relationships, accelerate CX Transformation and achieve increased and sustained revenue and profits. These are often frank and vital discussions about the challenges of deepening customer relationships, improving a brand's operations for better decision-making, and transforming a brand's customer knowledge management—in other words, real-world issues.

The conversations that you're about to read in this Part are open, wide-ranging discussions with leaders who are experts in CX. In reading about their experiences, you'll have a front-row seat to seeing CX Transformation in action. There is no better way to learn, to grow, to evolve than by listening to people who have had remarkable levels of success in the very arena that you're now entering. Thank-you to Deb Kerschen, to Danny Winokur, and to Adam Lebofsky for taking the time to share their CX experiences with us, and even more for the insights that they provided.

Chapter 13

The Importance of Leadership Guidance:

A Conversation with Deb Kerschen, Intel Corporation

You can't have a deep relationship if you're not authentic.

Deb Kerschen is a longtime champion of Customer Experience. Deb has worked primarily in the technology sector, spending the majority of her career at Intel, where she has held a series of successive senior positions managing contact centers, CX data collection, and social media. We first met Deb in 2006 and we've been engaged in a lively conversation about CX ever since. Most recently, we talked about the impact of leadership on CX success, as part of her role in overseeing post-sales Support.

Our research shows that brands at the highest level of CX Transformation are almost 2x more likely to have leaders who regularly apply customer knowledge to their decision-making and actions compared to brands at the lowest level. What role did leadership play in the CX Transformation efforts of companies like Intel?

Prior to CX Transformation, many organizations I worked with tended to be hyper-focused on the product cycle above all other considerations. CX was appreciated but, lacking executive attention, it never was able to become a business priority. Once leadership stepped in, it was possible to evolve this mindset change and to prioritize the customer.

A big challenge for brands is to identify a clear set of short- and long-term CX goals. Brands at the highest level of CX Transformation are 4x more likely to consistently set and update their CX priorities, in comparison with brands at the lowest level. Once Intel's leadership decided to prioritize CX Transformation, what was the first action they undertook?

Our company was biased in its own beliefs of what they "knew" customers wanted or should want. As a result, we weren't focused on the right questions, namely, "Hey, do you like this? How can this be better? Is it easy enough to obtain answers to your technical questions? What would make you want to buy more?" We just did what the product development groups decided, based only moderately, on what the Sales and Marketing organizations would offer as input. That was done without customer experience data to back up any of it.

Once leadership determined that customer relationships needed to be prioritized, the first thing that became clear was that we lacked the necessary knowledge of our customers' experiences. All we had previously were bits and pieces of data on spreadsheets, and everyone would argue over whose data was most relevant, which department owned what data, and whose data should be used for decision-making.

At long last, our organization decided to collect more and multi-dimensional customer data and to analyze it in order to glean customer knowledge. That is when things started to change. We hired ONR to oversee our Voice of Customer (VOC) research. Once that commitment was made, it was only a matter of time until the data revealed that every single customer support contact was an opportunity to drive a deeper relationship that would impact future sales.

How did digital and, more importantly, social media, impact your customer support organization?

Prior to the advent of social media, our customers' digital experience was wholly led by the sales and marketing organization and they were pre-occupied with creating splashy websites with cool graphics and making the brand more recognizable to the public. Support, honestly, was an afterthought, even though most of the visits to our websites were for obtaining technical support—over 75%, in fact. And the rise of social media changed the game for customer support. Now customers had the power to break companies. It was all out there in public, on customers' own websites and blogs, on Facebook, on Twitter. These were conversations that just couldn't be ignored. That's when customer support went to leadership with a plan to interject themselves into these brand conversations that were happening on social media without their participation. Thanks to influential data, customer support's influence began to be recognized clearly as a contributor to the sales and revenue cycle rather than a nuisance and an unwarranted cost at the end of the sales process.

What's the most important thing that a Brand can do to make its CX Transformation program successful?

Today, more than ever, a brand needs to be authentic. They need to walk their talk. Don't say "We're customer-centric," then make it difficult for a customer to easily access Support services. If your actions don't align with your words, then you create doubt in your customers' minds about what you really care about. That doubt can fester and undermine your relationship and, ultimately, your brand.

If a company does things that promote trust and commitment, it's building a genuine long-term relationship. When customers feel cared for before, during, and—believe it or not—after a purchase, the brand is creating the most value. You can't have a deep relationship without that authenticity.

ONR

Chapter 14

How to Successfully Evolve the Brand:
A Conversation with Danny Winokur, Adobe Inc.

CX is the new competitive currency.

Danny Winokur is a customer experience pioneer and software executive. He was most recently the general manager of AppDynamics, a hyper-growth, venture-backed SaaS unicorn acquired by Cisco for $3.7B in 2017, and previously served stints as chief product officer and chief customer officer. Before AppDynamics, he was instrumental in driving the wildly successful transformation of Adobe's core business from Creative Suite® to Creative Cloud®, with a focus on customer experience. Danny now advises venture-backed SaaS companies, on customer experience and product development.

As we were finalizing this book, we spoke with Danny about ways to measure Customer Experience.

What made Adobe change its direction and adopt a cloud-based subscription model and launch Creative Cloud?

Prior to launching Creative Cloud, Adobe was a typical product cycle-driven software business with a shrink-wrapped perpetual software product sold primarily through distributors and retailers. We released a new version approximately every 18 months and all the machinery of the company was oriented around this cycle and driving upgrades. We managed single-digit growth through pricing and packaging optimizations, but we had saturated our market of creative professionals willing to pay $1,000 and more for Creative Suite, and the business was stagnating. We needed a fundamental change to drive real growth. We recognized that we could transform the business by engaging with our customers directly and introducing subscription pricing that dramatically lowered the cost of entry for our products, while significantly increasing the frequency with which we could release new innovations.

What role did customer experience play prior to the launch of Creative Cloud?

Customer experience wasn't even a thing. We recognized that if we were going to engage our customers directly, we had to think about their experiences in a much more holistic way. Our website, adobe.com, trials of our core products like Photoshop® and Illustrator®, our training tutorials, and our customer support interactions were all now part of *one customer experience* that would determine whether our customers paid for another month of service as we shifted to a subscription model. This was a massive change of mindset across every aspect of our business. We had been used to relying on intermediaries for most of these interactions in the largely indirect business we had been running. Instead of siloed functions optimized to support third-party partners, we had to develop a shared focus on our end customers and the overall experience they were having with us. This became a rallying cry across Adobe that we focused on every day across all functions of the business with clear metrics to measure our success.

How did you measure your progress in transforming the business, and in particular, your success in building direct and deeper relationships with your end customers?

Offering our customers a way to enjoy the full value of the Creative Suite for as little as $49 per month with Creative Cloud, or even less for individual apps like Photoshop, was a big risk. If we didn't deliver value each month, customers could cancel and stop paying. This was also a great, closer to real-time, feedback mechanism for us. We became laser-focused on a few key metrics that were our monthly report card and told us whether we were delivering a good and valuable customer experience. The most important overall metric was Annual Recurring Revenue, or ARR, which was not well-understood at the time. It was a calculation of the annual value of the subscriptions to which our customers were currently committed, including both new subscribers and churn. Those were our important secondary metrics: new subscribers and churn. We began reporting quarterly ARR and subscriber count (net of churn) on our earnings calls. These were simple proxies for both the progress of our business transformation and the health of our increasingly direct customer relationships, and by extension, the customer experiences we were delivering.

So, you identified your key success metrics tied to your customers' experiences. Once these were in place, what did it mean for how you managed the business?

Increasing ARR meant delivering an exceptional customer experience. The first change for us was recognizing that every way we interacted with our customers was an important part of one overall experience that ultimately determined whether they subscribed and continued to pay. Making Photoshop great was still important, but the experience on adobe.com and the ability to try before buying were also really important, as were friendly tutorials to make customers productive with what can be complex applications, and the support experience if they needed help. If we were going to consistently improve ARR, we knew we needed to create internal accountability for the overall customer experience across all these previously disparate pre- and post-sales functional teams to integrate them into a seamless whole.

I took on the new role of General Manager for what we initially called "Customer Engagement," and later, "Customer Experience." We re-organized the business to create my new team: product development for Creative Cloud functions (e.g., the purchase experience, file/asset sync, account management, etc.) that spanned across the individual desktop applications (e.g., Photoshop, Illustrator, InDesign, etc.), the adobe.com website team, documentation and training teams, and customer support, including all our global call centers, as well as some "federal" authority over the collection of independent "states" that were our storied desktop apps (Photoshop, Illustrator, InDesign®, Acrobat®, etc.).

This was incredibly disruptive, as many of these teams had previously been part of other corporate organizations outside this business unit (e.g., marketing, IT, worldwide field operations) with different cultures, and with goals that were often centered on cost optimization. They did not think of themselves as core to the product and they certainly weren't used to working together with each other or with the teams that built our marquee desktop apps like Photoshop and Illustrator. Those desktop app teams were each strongly independent, and rightly very proud of the amazing applications and user communities they had built over many years. The leaders of both the corporate teams and the desktop app teams were less than excited to give up the control they had long enjoyed with great success to a new upstart "Creative Cloud Customer Engagement Team." Yet, we knew this had to happen if we were to achieve the unified focus on customer experience needed to optimize the try-buy-expand-renew funnel that drove up our ARR.

That is a fundamental re-imagining of the business. Our research shows that CX Transformation positively impacts employee satisfaction. In fact, brands at the highest level of CX Transformation are 4 times more likely to see significant improvements in employee satisfaction for their efforts compared to those at the lowest level. How did employees at Adobe react to this change?

Initially, there was the tension you would expect with such a big change. In a very short period of time, we had declared new measures of success, re-organized the business, and fundamentally shifted priorities and how and where decisions were made. Some employees were really excited and saw the opportunity. Others resisted the change and felt threatened. Many were in the middle—unsure what this all meant, uncomfortable with the relatively sudden uncertainty, and anxious to re-establish themselves.

Senior leadership alignment was critical to our success in powering through the internal resistance to change. From our board and CEO to all of our senior leadership team, there was visible alignment with conviction and a very clear, crisp, and repeated narrative that focused on benefits for all stakeholders: customers, employees, and investors. We were direct about being all-in on the change, and our leadership decisions and actions reinforced that commitment. Importantly, results quickly followed, as we began consistently meeting and beating quarterly ARR and subscriber growth targets. As our stock began to rise based on our ARR growth, most employees became enthusiastic about where we were going and the rewards they were receiving from a quickly rising stock price. From a starting price of $28.48 on January 5th, 2012, our stock price had reached $501.15 by

October 15th, 2020. (That's an increase of 1,750%, if you're interested!)

Alignment of our strategy, leadership messaging and actions, metrics, stock performance, and compensation created a very powerful and persuasive mix that won the day. Those employees who just could not adapt to the changes—and there were some—ultimately left the business, but the vast majority became enthusiastic advocates over the first couple of years of the transformation. This self-reinforcing flywheel—and the focus on customer experience—ultimately powered an incredible and pioneering cloud and business model transformation, at scale, while in the spotlight of the public markets.

How did the public markets react to this change in direction?

Our CEO and CFO had done a phenomenal job setting expectations that revenue and profits would decline for an extended period as we converted customers from paying us up front to paying much smaller per-month subscription fees that were both more predictable and expanded our addressable market. It was a tricky message on Wall Street, where valuations were largely based on traditional metrics and ARR was a little understood and new "calculated" value lacking rigor.

Our CFO provided analysts with a detailed financial model that showed the "stacking effect" of overlapping subscription cohorts over time as we converted perpetual customers to subscription and added net new customers because our products would be affordable to a much larger addressable market of customers. The model showed that over time, the initially strong downward pressure of the shift from up-front to ratable revenue recognition eventually gives way to the power of subscription stacking and market expansion. Together, they would drive revenues and profits higher than where we started, while also making them much "higher quality" because of recurring predictability.

Wall Street was enthusiastic about the potential but, of course, needed leading indicators that we were executing each quarter to achieve the long-term results promised by the model, even as our revenue and profits declined. ARR and Net New Subscriber growth served this purpose perfectly as the primary drivers of the model math. We built rigor around our definitions for both metrics and began reporting on them transparently every quarter. As they grew consistently quarter after quarter, the market developed confidence in our ability to execute the transformation and the long-term benefits of the subscription model expanded our multiple and drove stock performance. Our success not only rewarded our shareholders and employees, but also paved the way for many other businesses that followed in converting or building their business models and valuations on ARR.

What advice would you give brands that are looking to move past old-school indirect models to engage their end customers directly through digital experiences?

It doesn't matter what industry you're in—financial services, energy, transportation, healthcare, retail—your core business is conducted through digital systems, online applications, and your website, all of which affect how you interact with your end customers. The COVID-19 pandemic has only accelerated this transformation and ever-rising customer expectations for great digital experiences. Digital-native companies with user-centric design in their DNA—companies like Google, Amazon, Facebook, and Uber—are embedded in our lives and have helped to set the bar for digital experiences that we reflexively expect, whether in our roles as consumers or employees using enterprise applications.

Delivering a great digital customer experience is the new competitive currency and needs to be a core competency for every company. That has major implications for how most companies—those not born in the cloud—invest, organize themselves, develop metrics, and build design-centric development and operations teams focused on the end-to-end experience of their customers. It's imperative that leaders recognize this and re-invent themselves to prevent existential threats from other digital disruptors.

Chapter 15

The Value of a Plan:

A Conversation with Adam Lebofsky, JPMorgan Chase & Co.

Listen to what your customers are really telling you!

Adam Lebofsky, a Customer Experience evangelist, is an executive who works primarily in the Financial sector. He has served in a variety of roles, including marketing and operations, focusing primarily on customer-centric strategy and operations. Adam is currently Senior VP of Marketing at JPMorgan Chase. We were delighted to catch up with Adam recently and continue an ongoing discussion about the need for a comprehensive CX plan, albeit a flexible one in the current

COVID-19 environment, as a necessity for achieving organizational goals.

Brands at the highest level of CX Transformation are 5 times more likely to apply customer knowledge to guide their employee training and development activities compared to those at the lowest level of CX Transformation. As a JPMorgan Chase executive, what do you see as the biggest challenge to improving customer experience?

To use an analogy, if customer knowledge is off-the-field practice, and integrating this knowledge into our daily business actions is on-the-field success, our biggest challenge is integrating customer knowledge consistently into actions we take to achieve business success. Our goal, as it relates to CX Transformation, is to always be driving actions that improve customer experience by cost-effectively prioritizing our efforts and directing our energy and resources to areas most likely to improve CX.

JPMorgan Chase regularly delivers exceptional customer experience to over 80% of their customers, so you have been effective at driving on-the-field success. What's your secret to getting your teams to consistently integrate customer knowledge into actions?

In simple terms, to know customers deeply, you must always be attuned to improving your ability to collect feedback from them. Because broad, high-level customer experience metrics provide only a limited understanding of actual customer experience, the key is to be able to acquire enough of the right customer data so that we can transform data into customer knowledge. To accomplish this, we implemented a comprehensive listening plan that allowed us to hear what all segments of customers are saying wherever they may express themselves. And, importantly, we can do this at scale, not just for a segment.

Our research shows brands at the highest Level of CX Transformation are 5 times more likely than those at the lowest Level to use the customer knowledge they acquire to optimize customer journeys. How do you apply customer knowledge to help drive on-the-field success?

We analyze our CX data to find performance gaps that are customer experiences that are less than optimal. We choose to focus on resolving the issues of the dissatisfied customers as a means of raising overall performance while understanding that these only represent a small minority of our customers. We believe in going further as an organization, taking the extra steps necessary to identify those that fall outside our common path and often represent the dissatisfied few. The result is that all customers, even those that take an uncommon path, are not left behind.

So you have identified a set of customers who need special attention. What happens next?

Once a segment has been identified, we perform a root-cause analysis to understand what really happened and where the opportunities for improvement lie. To do this, we look at friction points within the context of the customer's entire journey. Questions are asked: Was the source of friction recent or did it occur earlier in a customer's journey? Through this exercise, we are able to arrive at a set of recommendations and then these recommendations need to be vetted and ultimately approved.

Once you've identified a problem with a segment and arrived at some recommendations, do you go straight to implementation?

No. Because we need to socialize and take advantage of our employees' customer knowledge to ensure we are embarking on the right actions. That's where the socialization process adds value. Recommendations are discussed, evaluated, improved, and iterated across teams and businesses, and up and down leadership ladders. We have found that effective socialization depends on full transparency about the problem, its cause and impact, the possible solutions and what they may require—vs. the cost of doing nothing.

Then we act!

This is a complex and inclusive process. How long did it take you to develop this approach?

This methodology evolved over time. But it started from the top and it was a top-down cultural decision that came straight from [Chairman & CEO] Jamie Dimon. He wanted a system that was both complementary to the rest of the organization and yet largely independent of it.

Our approach may appear linear when you examine it at a high level, but it's really a leveling up process in which our CX team faced similar challenges time and again as it moved through the system with improved knowledge, clearer priorities, and organizational alignment. All of which positions decision-makers to take action to root out dissatisfaction quickly so that the organization can effectively prioritize, take action, and move the needle on the whole.

PART V

Getting to the Payoffs: It's All About Balance and Momentum

Chapter 16

A conversation with Jason Ten-Pow

There is no one-size-fits-all solution to improving Customer Experience.

In theory, CX Transformation appears simple enough, so why do so many brands struggle to CX Transform?

The reason why most brands struggle can be traced to their approach to CX Transformation. Most leaders view it as a simple short-term problem to be solved and fail to give it the attention it deserves. It's something that can be managed, so you just create a team to resolve the issue, they do some work, they propose a solution, and then it's fixed and you move on to the next problem. This is wholly ineffective, of course.

So how should brands manage their customer relationships?

Like any other meaningful relationship, customer relationships need attention on an ongoing basis. It's so fundamental to any business: you just cannot afford to take your eyes off it. And it's not something that can just be fixed. Like any relationship, customer relationships need to be nurtured and appreciated. This means it requires significant and ongoing attention from every single member of the organization.

What do you tell leaders who think this will be an easy fix?

I usually start by explaining that deep relationships don't just happen. Brands must act consistently and intentionally to nurture relationships. After all, we know that humans are complex emotional beings with wants, needs, and desires. Relationships deepen when brands connect with customers on an emotional level while they are fulfilling these wants, needs, and desires.

So how should leaders approach CX Transformation?

To be honest, this involves nothing short of a cultural transformation. The brand must re-orient its decisions and actions in a way that prioritizes its customers. This requires a serious commitment by leadership, management, and the entire workforce. And it's not a linear process; rather, it's a leveling-up process, where the brand expands its CX Transformation efforts to embrace more and more decisions and actions across the entire business.

So CX Transformation is not about short-term problem solving; instead, it's a cultural transformation. But organizations will want to move quickly to CX

Transform; what is the risk of moving too quickly through the five Levels of CX Transformation?

There are significant risks that come with moving too fast or too slow. If you try to move too fast through the Levels, your employees' habits will not be re-oriented towards your customers in a truly meaningful and permanent way. For some employees, this needs new muscles; for others, their muscles are being re-used after a long period of non-use. Every department needs adequate time to acquire the appropriate muscle memory before you move to the next Level.

What is the risk of moving too slowly through the Levels of CX Transformation?

If you move too slowly, your organization can easily become distracted by other short-term priorities that deliver quicker, although smaller, payoffs. Believe it or not, taking too long to achieve an ROI for CX Transformation efforts is the surest way to lose momentum and ultimately stall CX Transformation.

So how do you achieve optimal momentum?

Those leading this effort must have the know-how to recognize when is the right time to move to the next Level in order to maintain momentum. It's really important to allow every department enough time to adopt and master each Level of CX Transformation. It's all about getting the balance right; only then will CX Transformation take place in an effective manner that maximizes the financial and organizational rewards.

How does leadership feel when optimal momentum is reached?

The brand feels like they and their customers are in sync, metaphorically holding hands, building trust and growing closer to one another. They are on the path to an unbreakable relationship.

Where do most brands find themselves when it comes to customer relationships?

Many, if not most, brands fail to know and understand customers. Competition may be driving a wedge into what was once a strong relationship. This is the messy middle where most brands are stuck. I see this as a tremendous opportunity and the rationale for CX Transformation.

It sounds like the CX Transformation process that each organization undertakes is unique to them.

Yes! It doesn't matter whether you're an established brand or a wholly new brand. There is no one-size-fits-all solution to improving Customer Experience. It's completely bespoke. And yet, there are recurring challenges brands will confront again and again. If a brand focuses on those challenges and has a clear methodology for overcoming them, then its potential is unlimited.

What advice would you give those considering CX Transformation?

Once a brand makes that commitment, then they are now moving beyond just hoping that a relationship will blossom. It's a reality that is now within arm's reach. At the early Levels of CX Transformation, don't let your enthusiasm for deeper customer relationships tempt you into over-investing too early in the CX Transformation process. Most brands don't start out with the knowledge that's needed to be able to make the right investments early on. Instead, if they follow the CX Transformation Playbook, they will complete the fundamentals and acquire the knowledge needed to make the investments that will deliver higher Levels of ROI. Once they reach the middle Levels, then they are better positioned to acquire the greater payoffs that align with the increased investments.

What are the payoffs for brands that reach the highest Levels of CX Transformation?

This is not a "feel good" exercise. As a brand moves from Level to Level, the likelihood that it will achieve significant payoffs grows dramatically. Our research compared brands that had reached the highest Level of CX Transformation with the brands that were only at the lowest Level. Those at the highest Level were 6 times more likely to see significant increases in revenues and profits, as a result of their CX Transformation efforts. But that's not all: those same brands were also 5 times more likely to experience significant improvements in organizational efficiency.

How can a brand get more information and insight into the value and ROI that it can expect from a well-implemented CX Transformation program?

For starters, I would point them to our website at <u>onrcx.com/ unbreakable</u>. They can also connect with us by email or through my LinkedIn profile page. Details are at the front of the book.

PART VI

Staying on Course:
Checkpoints for Leading a Successful CX
Transformation

Unbreakable. In a word, that's the end game. It's the relationship status that we aspire to for you—the pinnacle of CX. Our mission is to help you develop nothing short of unbreakable bonds with your customers. CX Transformation is the way to get there and by handing you our Playbook, we believe this is achievable.

Customer relationships are entirely conditional; their health and resiliency depend on a multitude of factors. What's more, they exist on a live continuum ranging "Ruptured," at one extreme, to "Unbreakable," at the other, And every single customer inter-action has the potential to move the needle in one direction or the other. Well, we know on which end of that continuum you'd like to see your brand.

The Playbook in Part III contains all the Steps involved in accomplishing a really successful CX Transformation, as your CoRE Team leads your organization through each Level.

During some 20-plus years of helping our clients navigate CX Transformation, we have learned that every organization is different. The challenges that your leaders will face at each Level of your CX Transformation journey will be unique, and your organization will need to find its own pace of progress that keeps everyone engaged and committed.

With that in mind, Part VI provides a set of checkpoints that will help you manage and maintain the pace of CX Transformation that is right for your organization.

Each **Checkpoint** is a specific question that helps you assess whether you're now ready to move forward.

Following each checkpoint, the **How** is a guide to what to look for when you're answering the question, "Are we ready to move to the next Level of CX Transformation?"

Checkpoints for Level 1

At the Planning Level of CX Transformation, your objective is to educate your C-suite about CX Transformation and lay the groundwork for the process.

Level 1 Playbook Steps Summary

1. Align Mission Statement with CX Values
2. Map it out
3. Manage expectations
4. Assign a CX Transformation Point Person
5. Embed Collect/Share/Act
6. Establish CX-specific KPIs

Checkpoint: *Has everyone bought into "Customer First?"*
How: Is there a shared enthusiasm for prioritizing the customer?

Enthusiasm among your leadership people for your Vision and Mission and what is possible should increase at every Step. Your objective is to solidify the primacy of your brand's customers at the top level and to ensure that all decisions and actions throughout the CX Transformation process align with your mission of deepening the relationships with your customers by delivering to their fully understood wants, needs, and desires.

Checkpoint: *Does your Leadership Team "Walk the talk"?*

How: Is your Leadership Team on board and involved with prioritizing your customers?

All members of the C-suite are now involved in ensuring that the organization is prioritizing its customers. It is already moving away from a singular focus on financial efficiency (which is still the CFO's reference point) and technology for technology's sake (the CTO/CIO's watch). The Leaders of Strategy, Marketing, Sales, and HR are becoming active participants with specific roles to play.

Leadership understands that CX Transformation can only succeed when all members of the C-suite work together.

Checkpoint: *Is everyone thinking proactively about adding customer metrics to scorecards?*

How: Is curiosity (and, perhaps, clarity) growing among the leadership team and department heads about how to measure their progress towards meaningful customer prioritization?

Questions about how to measure the success of individual departments are being raised more and more with each new Step. The C-suite starts to understand not only that there are both hard measurements (the KPIs) and soft measurements (knowledge of the customer) that will need to be tracked within each department, but also how these metrics support other departments. These questions should become more tactical with each new Step taken at Level 1.

Checkpoints for Level 2

At the Learning Level, you launch CX Transformation within post-sales. This is the brand's testing and learning ground where you optimize your approach before expanding across other departments.

Level 2 Playbook Steps Summary

1. CoRE Team
2. CoRE Team's mission
3. Customer priorities for post-sales support
4. Mind the gaps
5. KPIs for post-sales support

Checkpoint: *Is there excitement in the hallways about the CoRE Team—or politics?*
How: Are employees questioning the purpose of the CoRE Team?

Level 2 usually provokes a chorus of questions, even some push-back, about the purpose of the CoRE Team. There will be questions about why the Team's members are asking for specific details or even data about post-sales performance. You may even hear complaints that the CoRE Team is encroaching on other departments' territories. When you hear these questions and concerns, it is important to reassure your colleagues that the undertaking is not aimed at evaluating departmental performance; rather, that the goal is no more, and no less, than better understanding your customers' wants, needs, and desires. As long as the CoRE Team is doing a good job of educating (instead of intimidating) the post-sales departments, the volume of questions should reduce with each new Step.

Checkpoint: *Is the CoRE Team figuring things out and getting things done—or are they stuck?*
How: Do you have the right people in the right positions on the CoRE Team?

> Lack of tangible results is a tell-tale sign that the make-up of the CoRE Team is not balanced. The imbalance is usually the result of the team having too many strategic and not enough tactical workers (or vice versa). For the CoRE Team to be successful, it needs a balance of tactical team members who can dig deep into the problem, along with strategic thinkers who can synthesize the many micro issues to identify the macro-opportunity.

> Be on the lookout for two warning signs of CoRE Team imbalance. The first is an inability to acquire and align all of the CX data that is being collected; this is because you don't have enough tactical members. The second is the inability to make sense of the information that is being collected because you don't have enough strategic thinkers. If you see the CoRE Team running into either of these two problems, you need to step in and take corrective action by re-balancing the team membership.

Checkpoint: *Is the team listening for what's working and what's not, and are they sharing those stories with Leadership?*
How: Are members of the organization asking for KPIs or other assessment measures of progress?

> Establishing achievable expectations at this early Level of CX Transformation is super-important. While there will be pressure to achieve immediate payoffs for even these early efforts, it's important that anyone and everyone who seeks quick results understands that the really meaningful financial results will be felt when the program advances to the higher Levels. Patience is key; remember that the first person out of the starting blocks seldom wins the marathon.

At the same time, it is important to get some quick wins. One good way to do this is for the CoRE Team to focus on sharing customer knowledge that you may have uncovered in one part of a department with other members of that same department and ask them what actions they intend to take to improve "their" customers' experiences, based on this new-found knowledge. You may be able to move some KPIs by at least a few percentage points. While that is admirable in itself, what's even more important is acquiring and sharing stories about how increased customer knowledge has already started to change employees' actions. Seek out these stories actively and, even more importantly, record and re-tell them across your organization. With each new Step, you should be acquiring more and more of them.

Checkpoints for Level 3

At Level 3, you expand CX Transformation efforts to the pre-sales (Sales and Marketing) departments in order to improve the acquisition and sharing of customer knowledge. Once the pre- and post-sales functions start to share their own customer knowledge, they should become much better at coordinating their actions to begin to deepen customer relationships.

Level 3 Playbook Steps Summary

1. Expand your CoRE Team
2. Ignite collaboration
3. Optimize, using Collect/Share/Act
4. Focus on quality over quantity
5. Track employee CX decisions and actions

Checkpoint: *Is the CoRE Team getting better at its job?*
How: Are your inter-departmental processes coming into alignment?

At the beginning of Level 3, you will again face the same questions about the true purpose and intentions of your CoRE Team. More importantly, you need to be on the lookout for actions that improve alignment between departments. Are opportunities for optimization being brought forward and acted upon? Is duplicate work being identified and purged? With each new action, more and more impactful opportunities should be uncovered, and unnecessary redundancies removed.

Checkpoint: *Are the silos breaking down? Are departments working together?*
How: Are you seeing new partnership opportunities starting to appear?

Consolidating work items should now be happening. Instead of two separate departments working on the same problem, the CoRE Team should be helping to identify opportunities for partnerships between departments. There will be questions around who should fund what and why, so it's important to handle these questions tactfully to ensure that both parties have equal authority and accountability for the overall success of these partnerships. Foster and nurture these relationships, because they are a key step in tearing down department silos. You should be uncovering more of these opportunities as you move from Step to Step.

Checkpoint: *Are pre-sales and post-sales paddling in the same direction now?*
How: Are inter-departmental tensions declining?

Tensions will likely run high when you first bring departments together to tackle problems, if only because their methods and goals are probably very different, and each department will tend to push for theirs to predominate. It's important that departments align around the single organizational goal of deepening customer relationships, and put aside specific departmental goals. Let's face it; it's so much easier to encourage cooperation among <u>equals</u>. That's why it is so important to ensure that both departments are equally responsible for the success (or failure) of their collective efforts. The more clearly this mandate is explained and accepted, the fewer petty and momentum-slowing disagreements will emerge. With each additional Step, you should see an increasing level of trust between departments.

Checkpoints for Level 4

At Level 4, you take CX Transformation organization-wide. Now the rest of your brand joins the mission as you develop a solution to make it easy for your entire workforce to acquire and apply customer knowledge.

Level 4 Playbook Steps Summary

1. Expand your CoRE Team (again!)
2. Engage IT
3. Democratize your CX Data
4. Tracking Module for Employee CX decisions and actions

Checkpoint: *Is the CoRE Team doing their best to speed up? Is there a plan for moving ahead?*
How: Have short-term and long-term goals been set?

By the time your CX Transformation Program reaches Level 4, the CoRE Team will understand the complexity of its journey very clearly. It is important to use this knowledge, in connection with past experience, to carefully plan and prioritize the actions at this Level. Once again, the team will likely uncover planning and performance gaps and will need to go back and fix them, even while fielding demands to press on and move at a faster pace. If the greatest stumbling block at previous Levels was knowledge-gathering, then invest extra time to accomplish this task. If the greatest hurdle was education, then spend the time needed to educate the rest of the organization. At Level 4, you will start to see real payoffs for your CX Transformation efforts, but if you begin to rush the process or curtail how you plan and strategize, you could quickly undo the gains you have made. In short, this is the time to make sure the CoRE Team has a solid step-by-step plan, informed by their own experience, for rolling out CX Transformation to the entire organization.

Checkpoint: *Are you inviting more groups to the table? More than just the IT department?*
How: Are you taking a shortcut?

You are now faced with a significant investment as you combine digital and CX Transformation efforts. Your natural tendency is to trust IT to lead this process because they have come through for you in the past. It's an easy shortcut, but avoid this "safe play." Instead, balance responsibilities between the CoRE Team and IT, and make sure that the voices of all other departments in the organization are being heard. Why? Because you need the knowledge of how, when, and why this new system will be used to make your employees more knowledgeable about your customers and about the actions they must take to create those unbreakable relationships.

This is no longer about just delivering data; this is about educating your entire workforce. At the beginning of this process, you could well find yourself navigating through a minefield of differing opinions and perspectives. Don't discourage these discussions; rather, moderate them by reminding everyone at the table of the primary purpose of this Level—educating your entire workforce about "their" customers.

As the increasing focus on the customer begins to resonate within the design and development process, there will be greater alignment between all teams because their own objectives will also become aligned. It's when objectives are misaligned that tensions can start to escalate. At each Step, if you do not see a decline in tensions, that means the folks in the room are still not aligned on the primary objective of educating the entire workforce about their customers, so you'll need to step in and re-orient the team to this imperative.

Checkpoint: *Do more people want more data that they can do more with?*
How: Is the demand for CX data continuing to grow?

As you move through the Steps of Level 4, there will be a natural desire for more CX data. At every Step, departments will ask for new data, more data, and more frequent data. This is a natural outcome of the CX Transformation process, and these requests will have to be managed carefully. It's important to prioritize them to ensure that your teams are not deviating from their plan just to be seen to be accommodating every request. This will slow momentum. However, it is important to appreciate that the increased demand for CX data is a true indication that CX Transformation has taken hold.

Checkpoints for Level 5

You are now a leading brand, and you have achieved differentiation because of your commitment to CX Transformation. What now?

Checkpoint: *Is having more people involved making it faster? Or slower?*
How: Are you including a wider set of stakeholders in decision-making?

Look around and note the number of silos you have torn down with CX Transformation. Now it's important to continue this momentum by being ever more inclusive. No longer should there be the sense that there are two tiers of C-suite members: the inner circle of those who have the CEO's ear together with those who do not have this privilege). There should now be one unified leadership group with complementary roles designed and dedicated to ensuring the maintenance and deepening of customer relationships.

Checkpoint: *Are more decisions in more groups starting with more information about your customer?*
How: Do you feel that all departments are now effectively integrated and aligned?

Not only should the unified C-suite have a new-found sense of integration, but this should also be happening at the department level. There should be a stronger alignment around decisions and actions that flow from the organization's unwavering focus on the customer. Departments are working together more, and even when working independently, they are more aligned than ever in decision-making and actions.

Checkpoint: *Are you seeing more ideas coming from more groups with more data?*
How: Is there a surge in idea generation?

Well-thought ideas are being generated at an ever-increasing pace. Each idea is accompanied by recommendations for action and supported with credible and relevant customer data. These ideas are brought to the table with increasing levels of multi-departmental support, together with a clear focus on how they will have a positive impact on customer relationships. These are the types of activities that you will want to continue to foster and reward as you stay on your never-ending journey of creating unbreakable customer relationships!

Glossary

Brand

This term is used throughout this book in either of 2 senses:

(i) brand—to denote any business or organization, large or small, that is in business to acquire revenue and profits and which has a consistent image in the marketplace.

(ii) Brand—to denote a specific product or line of products that have a distinguishing image in the marketplace.

Customer Experience (CX)

Describes how a customer relates to a brand or business. CX is an emotional reflection of how the customer perceives, reacts to, and evaluates a brand, based on their entire relationship with it, and is the sum of all of their interactions with the brand.

Relationships between the brand and its customers exist on a customer relationship continuum. The weakest relationships are easily ruptured, while the strongest are unbreakable.

Customer Interaction

This is a single point of contact between a customer and the brand. Interactions may take many forms, including in-person, telephone, or online experiences

Customer Knowledge

Ideally, it is the accumulation of customer data and insights, collected from real interactions across various sources, analyzed and assembled in a logical and succinct manner. It provides a clearer understanding of customers' wants, needs, and desires.

In practice, Customer Knowledge is often, at best, "what we think we know about our customers, based on the limited data that we have collected about them so far."

Customer Loyalty

The customer's dedication to purchasing the same product or service repeatedly. This is not always based on a deep relationship; it can be based on convenience, or habit, or lack of alternatives. Loyalty is measured by the act of re-purchase, and the level of connection between re-purchasing and a strong relationship is *assumed*.

Customer Relationship Continuum

Like all relationships, the relationship between a brand and its customers is constantly evolving. The evolution of that relationship is measured on the Customer Relationship Continuum. The weakest relationships are easily ruptured, while the strongest are unbreakable.

CX Transformation

Customer Experience Transformation is the systematic approach to re-orienting a brand's priorities so that it aligns more closely with its customers' wants, needs, and desires.

CX Transformation is a 5-Level process that moves a brand along the customer relationship continuum towards developing unbreakable relationships. At each new Level, priorities come into closer alignment and relationships deepen, resulting in significant growth in revenue and profits.

Digital Transformation

Digital Transformation is the adoption of digital technology to transform services or businesses through replacing non-digital or manual processes with digital processes, and/or by replacing older digital technology with newer digital technology.

Optimize

Throughout this book, Optimize means, "To make the best possible use of ... ," or "To make as perfect, effective or functional as possible."

Pre-sales

This term typically includes the Sales and Marketing functions. The pre-sales mission is to encourage customers to purchase, re-purchase and share their experience of the brand with others. In CX terms, these are your brand's efforts to persuade and influence your customers while increasing customers' trust that your brand will do right by them.

Post-sales

These are the people who are communicating directly with your existing customers and are receiving direct customer feedback. They are the people most likely to be effective advocates for your customers.

Reorientation

The process of reorienting a brand's focus on its customers.

References

Harvard Business Review Article

What 575 C-Level Executives Really Think About CMOs

https://hbr.org/2019/09/what-575-c-level-executives-really-think-about-cmos

Deloitte Article

The confident CMO: 3 ways to increase C-suite impact

https://www2.deloitte.com/us/en/pages/chief-marketing-officer/articles/confident-cmo-c-level-communication-impact.html

ONR CX Transformation Research

Contents

Research Objective

Research Methods

Key Findings

Tables

Charts

Research Objective

To determine the impact of CX Transformation on overall business success.

Research Methods

- We used online quantitative surveys and telephone qualitative interviews to collect data.
- 1,000 online surveys and 50 qualitative interviews were completed between January 2019 and January 2021.
- Respondents were sourced from a professional online panel along with ONR's global network of executives.
- Quota sampling was employed to ensure a minimum number of surveys for key audiences.
- The average time to complete the survey was 14 minutes.
- The in-depth telephone interviews typically lasted for about one hour.

Using our proprietary algorithm, we identified each brand's current Level of progress through the 5 Levels of CX Transformation, based on:

- The comprehensiveness of the customer data that they collected;
- How widely they shared CX insights and knowledge across their organization;
- How extensively customer knowledge was used to inform decisions and actions.

Key Findings

- Two-thirds of brands were found to be at the 2 lowest Levels of CX Transformation, while only 6% of brands were at the highest Level.
- Brands that had achieved the highest Level of CX Transformation reported significant differences between themselves and competing brands in key areas, including revenue and profits.

- Brands that had achieved the highest Level of CX Transformation also reported significant differences between themselves and competing brands in terms of ROI for their CX investments across a number of key areas, including revenue, profits, internal efficiency, employee satisfaction and, of course, customer satisfaction.
- The higher the Level of CX Transformation, the more accurately leaders assessed their own Level of CX Transformation.
- Brands that aligned Digital and CX Transformation efforts reported that they had higher revenues and profits compared to their competitors than brands that did not align these efforts.

Quantitative Research: Summary of Respondents

Respondent's Job Role	Percent
Owner / Partner	13%
Chief Executive Officer	22%
Chief Financial Officer	12%
Chief Human Resources Officer	2%
Chief Information / Technology Officer	15%
Chief Marketing Officer	10%
Chief Operating Officer	8%
President / Senior Vice President / Vice President	3%
Head of business unit	2%
Head of department	5%
Senior Director / Director reporting directly to the C-suite	8%

Table 1   © ONR CX Transformation Research

Organization's Annual Revenue Range	Percent
$10 million to less than $50 million	7%
$50 million to less than $100 million	8%
$100 million to less than $200 million	8%
$200 million to less than $500 million	12%
$500 million to less than $1 billion	27%
$1 billion to less than $5 billion	27%
$5 billion or more	11%

Table 2   © ONR CX Transformation Research

Industry	Percent
Automotive	2%
Banking & Securities	14%
Consumer Packaged Goods / Services	5%
Health Care	12%
Industrial Products and Services	5%
Insurance	6%
Investment Management	5%
Life Sciences	5%
Media	5%
Mining	1%
Oil & Gas	4%
Pharmaceuticals	5%
Power & Utilities	5%
Retail, Wholesale & Distribution	5%
Shipping & Ports	3%
Technology	12%
Telecommunications	5%
Travel, Hospitality & Services	1%

Table 3 © ONR CX Transformation Research

Business Type	Percent
Business To Consumer	52%
Business To Business	35%
Direct To Consumer	13%

Table 4 © ONR CX Transformation Research

Organization's Level of CX Transformation

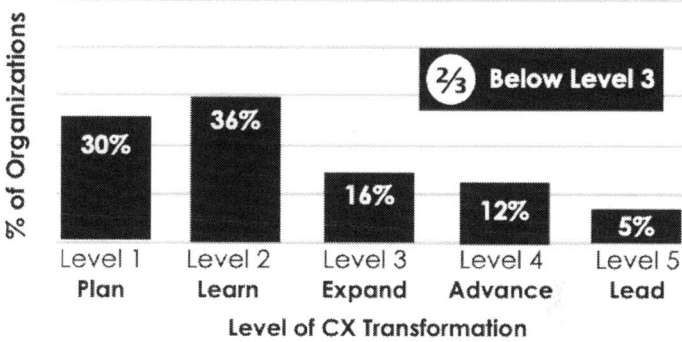

% of Organizations

⅔ **Below Level 3**

Level 1 Plan	Level 2 Learn	Level 3 Expand	Level 4 Advance	Level 5 Lead
30%	36%	16%	12%	5%

Level of CX Transformation

Chart 1   © ONR CX Transformational Research

Organizations with revenue significantly above industry average over the past 24 months

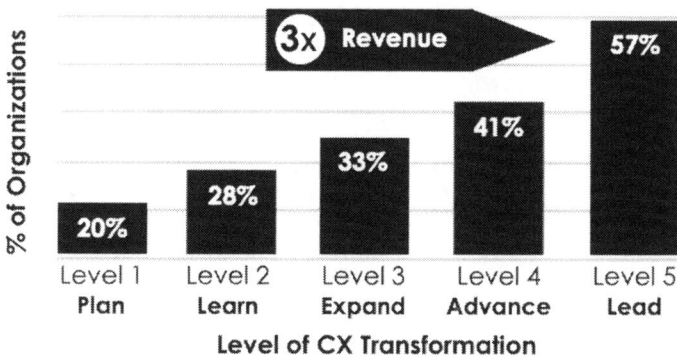

% of Organizations

3x Revenue

Level 1 Plan	Level 2 Learn	Level 3 Expand	Level 4 Advance	Level 5 Lead
20%	28%	33%	41%	57%

Level of CX Transformation

Chart 2   © ONR CX Transformational Research

**Organizations with profits significantly
above industry average over the past 24 months**

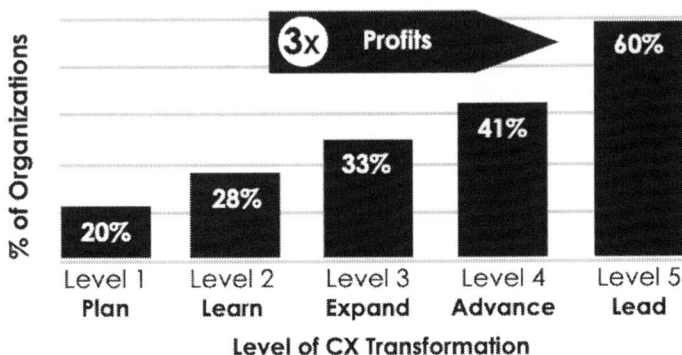

% of Organizations

3x Profits

| Level 1 Plan | Level 2 Learn | Level 3 Expand | Level 4 Advance | Level 5 Lead |
| 20% | 28% | 33% | 41% | 60% |

Level of CX Transformation

Chart 3

© ONR CX Transformational Research

**Organizations that accurately assessed their
level of CX Transformation**

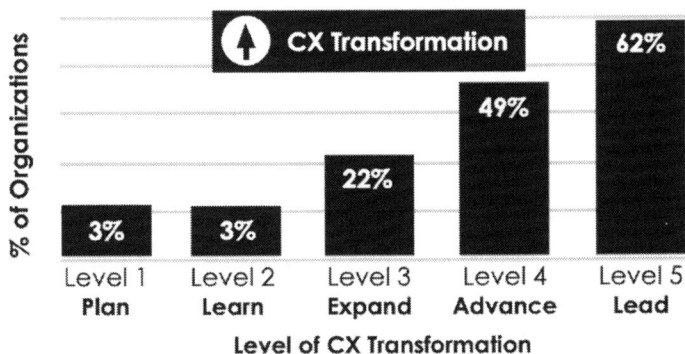

% of Organizations

CX Transformation

| Level 1 Plan | Level 2 Learn | Level 3 Expand | Level 4 Advance | Level 5 Lead |
| 3% | 3% | 22% | 49% | 62% |

Level of CX Transformation

Chart 4

© ONR CX Transformational Research

Organizations that achieved a significant improvement in organizational efficiency

Chart 5   © ONR CX Transformational Research

Organizations that achieved a significant improvement in revenue

Chart 6   © ONR CX Transformational Research

**Organizations that achieved a
significant improvement in profits**

Chart 7   © ONR CX Transformational Research

**CEOs who apply customer knowledge
to their decision-making**

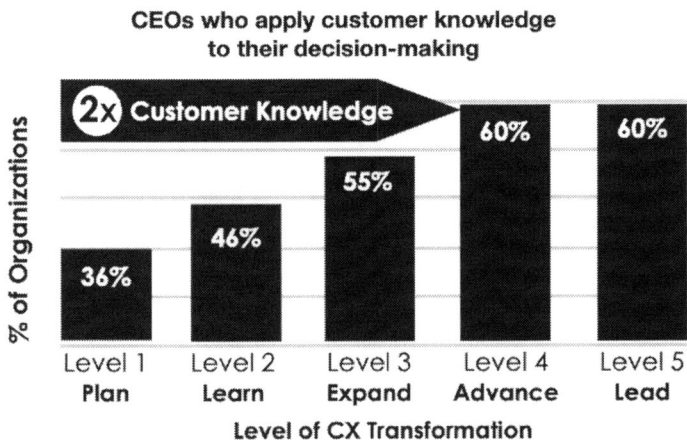

Chart 8   © ONR CX Transformational Research

**Organizations that have clear
short- & long-term CX goals**

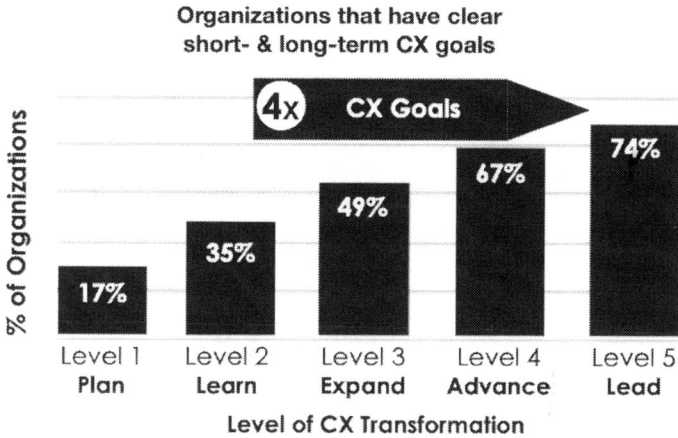

CX Goals — 4x

Level	% of Organizations
Level 1 — Plan	17%
Level 2 — Learn	35%
Level 3 — Expand	49%
Level 4 — Advance	67%
Level 5 — Lead	74%

% of Organizations (y-axis)

Level of CX Transformation (x-axis)

Chart 9   © ONR CX Transformational Research

**Organizations that have achieved a significant
increase in employee satisfaction as a result of
their CX Transformation efforts**

Employee Satisfaction — 4.5x

Level	% of Organizations
Level 1 — Plan	15%
Level 2 — Learn	26%
Level 3 — Expand	41%
Level 4 — Advance	65%
Level 5 — Lead	67%

% of Organizations (y-axis)

Level of CX Transformation (x-axis)

Chart 10   © ONR CX Transformational Research

Organizations that use customer knowledge to inform employee training and development

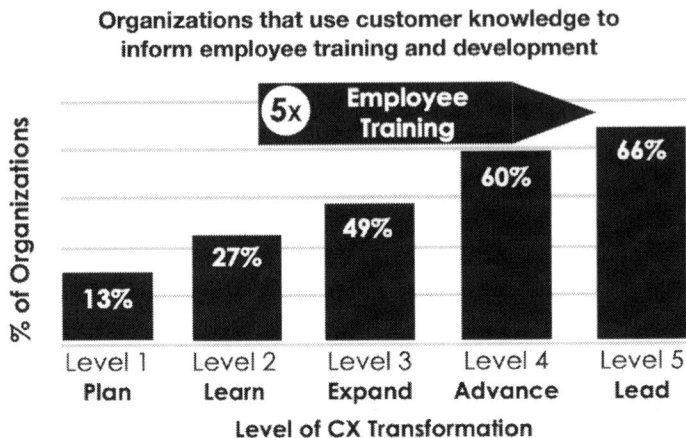

5x Employee Training

- Level 1 **Plan**: 13%
- Level 2 **Learn**: 27%
- Level 3 **Expand**: 49%
- Level 4 **Advance**: 60%
- Level 5 **Lead**: 66%

% of Organizations / Level of CX Transformation

Chart 11 © ONR CX Transformational Research

Organizations that use customer knowledge to optimize customer journeys

5x Customer Journey

- Level 1 **Plan**: 16%
- Level 2 **Learn**: 36%
- Level 3 **Expand**: 57%
- Level 4 **Advance**: 66%
- Level 5 **Lead**: 79%

% of Organizations / Level of CX Transformation

Chart 12 © ONR CX Transformational Research

Organizations that have achieved a significant increase in revenue as a result of their CX Transformation efforts

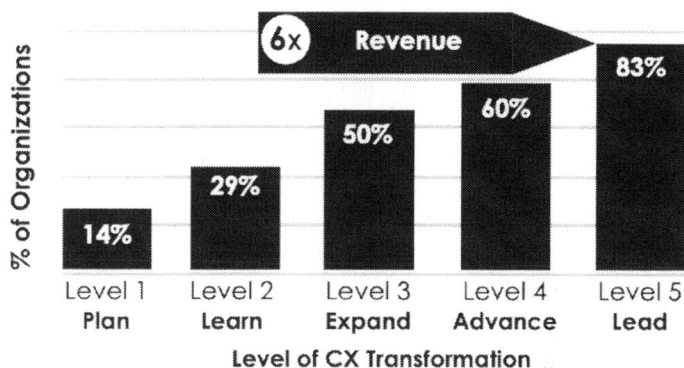

Chart 13   © ONR CX Transformational Research

Organizations that have achieved a significant increase in profits as a result of their CX Transformation efforts

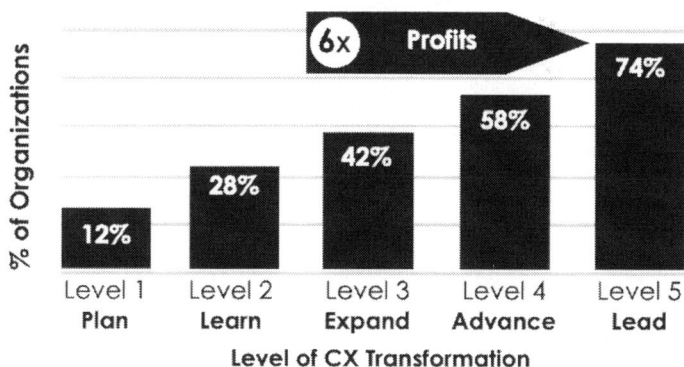

Chart 14   © ONR CX Transformational Research

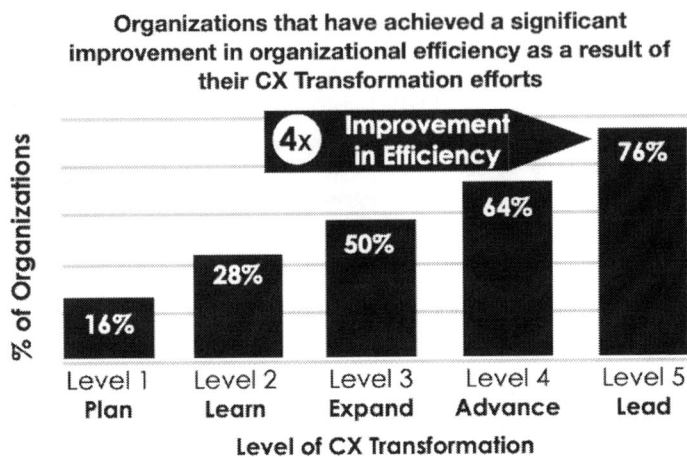

Organizations that have achieved a significant improvement in organizational efficiency as a result of their CX Transformation efforts

% of Organizations

4x **Improvement in Efficiency**

16%
28%
50%
64%
76%

| Level 1 | Level 2 | Level 3 | Level 4 | Level 5 |
| Plan | Learn | Expand | Advance | Lead |

Level of CX Transformation

Chart 15 © ONR CX Transformational Research

Author Biography
Jason Ten-Pow

The son of immigrants, Ten-Pow moved to Canada with his family when he was seven years old. As a teenager, his passion for customer experience was sparked as he worked behind the meat counter of a carnival-themed grocery store in Toronto, Ontario.

He earned his undergraduate degree in Political Science from the University of Toronto in 1996, where he developed a passion for studying voting behavior, and then he went on to York University for his master's degree, specializing in Quantitative Methods. As a student, Ten-Pow co-ran a small computer technology company, Visionary Enterprises, that built and installed computers and networks. This early venture taught him the basics of running a business and gave him the confidence to launch ONR, his CX consulting firm, of which he is the Founder and President, in 2001.

Under Ten-Pow's leadership, ONR has helped blue-chip companies such as Intel, Deloitte Consulting, and Coca-Cola, build and maintain strong relationships with customers.

Ten-Pow's years of helping companies improve their customer relationships have taught him that successful brands are able to differentiate through the process of Customer Experience Transformation (CX Transformation). Business leaders who use this approach have been consistently successful in acquiring deeper customer knowledge, which they use to re-prioritize their decision-making and actions to better align with the wants, needs, and desires of their customers.

Today, Ten-Pow has expanded his lifetime pursuit of helping brands develop unbreakable customer relationships by creating the Collect/Share/Act method for accelerating CX Transformation. This approach includes a suite of solutions that help brands **COLLECT** better CX data and **SHARE** customer knowledge more effectively across their organizations, so that they can **ACT** in closer alignment with the wants, needs, and desires of their customers. Using this approach, brands are able to quickly and efficiently differentiate themselves in a way that leads to a sustained increase in revenues and profits, together with improved organizational efficiency and employee satisfaction.

Ten-Pow released his first book, *UNBREAKABLE*, in the Spring of 2021, in which he pulls back the curtain on brands that seem to effortlessly build and maintain strong relationships with customers, and lays out a path for any company to do the same.

Ten-Pow spends time in both Toronto and Orlando with his son Ronin.

You can connect with Jason Ten-Pow via these links:

linkedin.com/in/jtenpow

@JasonTenPow

Jason.tenpow@onrcx.com

onrcx.com/unbreakable

Acknowledgments

Well, I did it. I've written my first book. It was a challenging process that was made easier (read "possible") because of the help and support I received from so many people.

I am grateful to Kirk Thompson, who said to me, "you should write a book," and then helped me turn my passion for customer experience into the book you are reading.

I am grateful to Seth Weiss for contributing to *UNBREAKABLE* and for his constructive feedback throughout the writing process.

I want to thank Anne O'Hagan, who took my drafts, notes, and verbal downloads and turned them into a complete and fluid manuscript.

I want to thank John Breeze for his careful and thoughtful editing.

A special thanks to Kevin Lau for leading the development team for Bespoke, ONR's proprietary CX Transformation product.

Thank you to Rye Asuro, Matt Ryan, and the entire ONR Team for their work supporting *UNBREAKABLE*.

I am appreciative of those who agreed to be interviewed for the book. I am incredibly grateful to those who shared detailed stories about customer experience. Thank you, Adam Lebofsky and Deb Kerschen.

I am additionally grateful to Danny Winokur, not only for his interview, but also for his review and feedback on the early manuscript.

I am grateful for the unwavering support of my mentor and friend, Anup Bansal.

There are many moments that have left an indelible mark on me and have ultimately influenced this book indirectly. The hockey teams that I played for, captained, coached, and managed are a big part of that. Thank you to all those who made playing hockey both enjoyable and educational.

I am thankful for my first job at Super Carnival, where I saw first-hand the value of being a customer-oriented business. I wouldn't say I liked the uniform, but the lessons I learned put me on a path that I continue to explore today.

There are many others whose support, guidance, and encouragement got me to the point where I could author a book. I would like to gratefully acknowledge Sita Ten-Pow (my mother), Fred Ten-Pow (my father), Rick Ten-Pow (my brother), Dawn Forsyth (my sister), Deanna Nunley, Becky Brown, and Gregory Yee.

And to the brightest light in my life, my son, Ronin.

Made in the USA
Middletown, DE
17 May 2021